The Grid For Supervisory Effectiveness

BY

Robert R. Blake and Jane Srygley Mouton

Austin, Texas U.S.A.

First printing January 1975
Second printing April 1976

Books by Dr. Robert R. Blake
and Dr. Jane Srygley Mouton:

CORPORATE EXCELLENCE THROUGH GRID®
ORGANIZATION DEVELOPMENT

THE MANAGERIAL GRID®

MANAGING INTERGROUP CONFLICT IN INDUSTRY
(with Herbert A. Shepard)

CORPORATE DARWINISM
(with Warren E. Avis)

GROUP DYNAMICS: KEY TO DECISION MAKING

BUILDING A DYNAMIC CORPORATION THROUGH
GRID® ORGANIZATION DEVELOPMENT

THE GRID® FOR SALES EXCELLENCE

HOW TO ASSESS THE STRENGTHS AND WEAKNESSES
OF A BUSINESS ENTERPRISE

THE MARRIAGE GRID®

INSTRUMENTED TEAM LEARNING T.M.

CONSULTATION

DIARY OF AN OD MAN

PREFACE

The Grid for Supervisory Effectiveness has been prepared to help supervisors at the first and second levels to increase their effectiveness.

The Grid is a way of learning about styles of supervision. Rather than outlining "one best way" and leaving it at that, the Grid permits you to study five quite different strategies of supervision. Then you can make the choice as to which strategy is best for you and your situation. In this way the Grid helps you sort out the alternatives, see the options that are available, and weigh the strengths and weaknesses of each.

Much research has been carried out in evaluating the styles of supervision identified by the Grid. Beyond that, applications of the Grid on an incompany basis, from wage earners through front line supervisors to middle and upper level managers, and including presidents and chief executives, have been conducted. This research and these application projects lead to definite conclusions as to how people want to be supervised and how supervisors want to exercise supervision. Since the research and field studies are evaluated elsewhere, only the summary will be presented here.[1] Our interpretation is that they lead to a basic conclusion. The 9,9 style gets the best results, produces the greatest involvement and commitment, and leaves the fewest undesirable side effects.

You may or may not reach similar conclusions yourself. What matters most is that you are aware of and understand the alternative modes of supervision. Then you can make your own choices, as no one can tell you what's best for you.

Writing *The Grid for Supervisory Effectiveness* has been a stimulating project. It provided us a chance to review our earlier conclusions and to formulate their implications for the first and second levels of supervision. Our aim has been to focus

---

[1]Blake, Robert R., and Jane Srygley Mouton. *Corporate Excellence Through Grid Organization Development.* Houston: Gulf Publishing Company, 1968.

attention on main issues rather than to prepare a highly detailed book or one that deals with issues of human effectiveness important at higher levels of management. These are written about elsewhere.[1]

Reginald C. Tillam contributed significantly to the entire project.

Robert R. Blake
Jane Srygley Mouton

January 1, 1975

[1]Blake, Robert R., and Jane Srygley Mouton. *The Managerial Grid*. Houston: Gulf Publishing Company, 1964.

TABLE OF CONTENTS

CHAPTER 1

The Grid For Supervisory Effectiveness

Dramatic changes are occurring in the way people handle their affairs. This is very much part of the situation within commercial firms, government agencies, schools and universities.

THE BREAKDOWN OF AUTHORITY AND OBEDIENCE

In the past, bosses exercised work-or-starve authority over their subordinates. They expected and got obedience from them. Authority-obedience was the basis for supervision that built pyramids, big ships, great armies, and made Prussia famous.

But authority-obedience as a way of life has became more and more objectionable as a basis for getting people to cooperate. Its defects can be seen most clearly when "everybody's doing it" authoritatively and demanding that others obey. In effect, many are rejecting traditional authority and trying to set up and act upon their own.

Yet the authority of the law is still established and appealed to as citizens, their representatives, and their governments seek improvements in many different areas. Legislation forced organizations to be more responsible for the safety of their employees, their customers, and the ordinary citizen as well. All this new-found social justice was for some years accompanied by affluence. In comparison with the old days, many young people now have a standard of living that has wiped out the need others felt in past decades to "buckle under" in order to survive. Even though circumstances of difference may shift, it is unlikely that those who have rejected authority-obedience as a way of life will readily accept it even if conditions of deprivation prevail.

OPTIONS FOR SUPERVISION

These many influences tell us that as far as bosses and subordinates are concerned, authority and obedience is no longer the only name of the game. Yet there still are bosses and subordinates inside organizations, and customers and citizens on the outside. What are their options?

The big question here, though, is how to be an effective supervisor. There are several major possibilities. We will explore each of them in this text.

One of these styles of supervision has more going for it than the others. This is the situation where the relationship between a boss and a subordinate is such that they can reach mutual understanding and agreement as to the course of action to be taken, as well as how to go about it. Even though the boss is still invested with the authority of his job responsibility, he seeks other means to accomplish results which yield increased effectiveness and positive gratification of those he supervises.

BARRIERS TO CHANGE

The shiftover from authority-obedience to involvement-participation-commitment has been slow in coming. It faces many difficulties. Here are just a few that might be mentioned. Most hark back to authority-obedience as somehow better, or more realistic, or more appropriate.

The first is evident among some bosses who disagree with this new approach. It conflicts with some of their most basic ideas about "how to run things." Bosses who disagree with involvement-participation-commitment say it's the responsibility of subordinates to carry out in a loyal manner what bosses tell them to do. Only then, they claim, is it possible to get the work out. Many bosses still see this way of supervising as The Right Way to work. They came up through the school of hard knocks and it made men out of them. If it was able to do that, they reason, there's not a whole lot wrong with it.

A further barrier to using involvement-participation-commitment is that the needed support of those who run the organization at the top is often lacking. The top people say, "Results are what count. It's your job to get them. Don't bother us with details." These attitudes reinforce the old authority-obedience formula. They encourage supervisors to go about doing things as they have in the past, that is, demanding results. The other difficulty with involvement-participation-commitment is seen in the argument that while "it may fit other situations, it's not for us; it just doesn't fit."

Still another blockage is that getting genuine involvement, participation, and commitment is viewed as taking up too much time. All the discussion and working through of reservations and doubts and uncertainties, and the need to clarify confusions and misunderstandings that is required, seem too great a task to tackle. Starting up a new involvement-participation-commitment approach is often very time-consuming. The argument is, "This might be the best way to manage if we had all the time in the world, but we don't. Action is needed now. If we stop to try to get understanding and agreement of each point along the way, we'd never get anything done."

Possibly the greatest difficulty is that the skills needed for supervising work in an involvement-participation-commitment way are scarce. These are skills of face-to-face interaction. They involve such things as getting agreement on what the real problem is that *needs* to be solved in any given case; listening for reservations and doubts rather than for signs of compliance; getting people to express their different views; and when disagreement has been polarized, dealing with conflict in an open and candid way to resolve it rather than to produce a winner and a loser or drive the disagreement underground or compromise the difference. However, it could be that time invested early in the process of working through these difficulties will pay great dividends later on when coordination in really fast-moving situations meshes together like that of a practiced sports team driving toward the goal line.

Before coming to any conclusions, though, we need to study *all* the main alternative ways of supervising. In Chapter 2 we will examine how management and supervision occur under an authority-obedience system and study its strengths and weaknesses. Chapter 3 considers the warmth and approval proposition, where the boss says, "If my subordinates like me, they'll do what I want without my having to tell them." Chapter 4 is about those hard-to-notice supervisors who are doing the least amount to get by on a "see no evil, speak no evil, hear no evil" basis. Chapter 5 describes the "halfway is far enough" supervisor who deals with problems by compromise, adjustment, and accommodation of differences by being willing to do what's "practical." Chapter 6 develops the possibility already introduced: seeking excellence in supervision through getting the highest possible involvement-participation-commitment to organization purpose up and down the line.

THE GRID

The Grid is a way of sorting out all these possibilities and seeing how each compares with the others. What is involved is this.

The Grid, as shown in Figure 1, clarifies and crystallizes many of the different possible ways you can supervise. Here is the basis of it. Anyone who is working for an organization has some assigned responsibilities. This is true whether he works very low on the job ladder or higher up. There are two matters on his mind whenever he acts as a manager or supervisor. One is *production*—getting results or accomplishing the task. How intensely he thinks about results can be described as his degree of concern for production. It is a nine-point scale where 9 shows high concern for production and *1*, low concern.

THE SUPERVISORY GRID

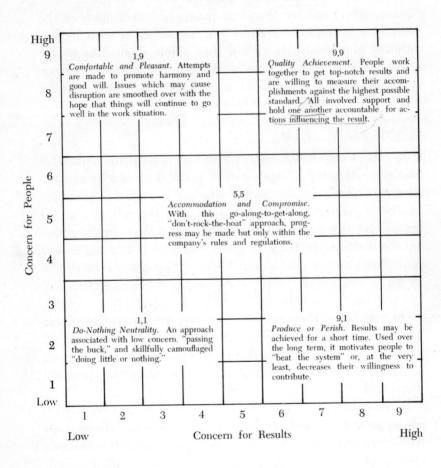

A supervisor also thinks about those whose work he directs because he has to get results through people. The Grid's vertical axis represents his concern for people. This too is a nine-point scale with 9 a high degree and 1 a low degree.

The Grid identifies these two concerns. It does so in a way that enables a person to see how the two concerns interact. Various "theories" are found at points of intersection of the two scales. Whether he realizes it or not, these are theories that different supervisors use when they think about how to get results through people. Five of the many possible theories or styles of supervision stand out most clearly. They appear in the four corners and in the center of the Grid.

GOING AROUND THE GRID

As can be seen in the lower right corner, 9,1 is the authority-obedience theory. It represents a great deal of concern for output but little for the people who are expected to produce. At the opposite corner of the Grid, the top left, is the 1,9 theory. It's the warmth and approval approach. In the lower left Grid corner is 1,1. It might seem odd that a supervisor could have almost no concern for either production or people by going through the motions of being part of an organization but not really contributing to it. Such supervisors do exist. Until you know their theory, they may be easy to overlook. They are not doers but freeloaders. They get by on a "see no, hear no, speak no evil" basis. They have not physically quit, but they've walked out of the company mentally, perhaps many years ago.

In the center of the Grid is the 5,5 style. The supervisor with this approach is going up the middle of the road. His attitude is, "Get results but don't kill yourself. Don't push too much or you will be seen as a *hard nose*. Don't let people off too easily or they will think you are *soft*. Be *fair but firm*. Do the job but find a comfortable tempo." The 5,5 manager is an "organization man."

The upper right corner, the 9,9 position, is high concern for production united with high concern for people. A person who supervises according to this theory stresses understanding and agreement through involvement-participation-commitment as the key to solving boss-subordinate problems. Whenever disagreements arise, he digs into the facts. The problem is thrashed through to solution in an open and aboveboard way that can result in mutual understanding with full commitment to conclusions reached. People working together in a 9,9 manner know that they have a common stake in the outcome of their endeavors. They mesh effort in an interdependent way. The 9,9 theory doesn't abide by the laws of arithmetic. On the joining of contributions, "one" plus "one" can add up to "three."

You probably have figured out that there are eighty-one combinations of concerns represented on the Grid. Next to 9,1 are 8,2 and 7,3. And 1,9 has 2,8 and 3,7 near it. There are 3,3; 4,4; 6,6; 7,7 along the diagonal between 1,1 and 9,9, and so on. But the main emphasis is on the theories in the corners and at the middle of the Grid. These are the most distinct styles. They're the ones you see most often. But you might think of a Grid style as you do shades of hair—black, brown, red, blond, and white. Within each hair shade there's a variety, yet on your driver's license the outstanding feature is enough for identification. The five main Grid styles, too, are broadly descriptive. We'll use them in much the same way. While talking about 9,1, remember it's just a tinge away to 8,2 or 7,3, or a halftone or so to 6,4, but all these neighboring combinations describe behavior in broadly similar ways.

Grid theories are described as sets of basic assumptions under which people deal with one another. An *assumption* is what you take for granted as being true or reliable. Maybe you learned most of your assumptions as you grew up. "I have to be . . . (a tough character or nice fellow) . . . to get what I want," illustrates some assumptions that persist. Supervisors act on the assumptions they hold even though it may be rare for any given supervisor to put them into words. The same set of assumptions usually underlies a whole range of attitudes and activities. For example, a 1,9-oriented boss who wants to please his subordinate may be quite inventive in finding all sorts of ways to show his own personal warmth. His behavior may not be so simple as to say "I appreciate you and everything you do" several times a day, but, nonetheless, keeping the subordinate happy dominates his thoughts and concern. His subordinate might say, "I never know what nice surprise the boss will think up next," and yet the supervisor's core assumptions are remarkably consistent—to avoid unpleasantness and to win the appreciation of his subordinates.

Assumptions are a necessary part of supervision. Were a person to act without assumptions, his behavior would be random, purposeless; it would *make no sense* in any predictable way. Even so, it is not enough just to *have* a set of assumptions. Faulty assumptions can ruin a supervisor. More reliable ones can enhance his work and enrich his life on the job as well as elsewhere. When a person acting under any set of assumptions understands them, this Grid knowledge can aid him to predict what the impact of his behavior will be on his colleagues and subordinates. Thus, learning the Grid framework will help you to understand what kinds of actions are likely to lead to what kind of results.

"DOMINANTS" AND "BACKUPS"

Does a supervisor have just one Grid style strategy or does he skip over the Grid, shifting and adapting according to how he sees the situation?

All but a very few supervisors have characteristic styles. This is his *dominant* style. Each boss' basic approach resembles one that is founded on either 9,1; 1,9; 5,5; 1,1; or 9,9 assumptions. But how can the idea that a person has a dominant Grid style square with the fact that people do shift and change? It can be understood in the following way. Not only does a supervisor have a dominant style, but he has a backup and sometimes a third strategy he falls back on. He uses a backup strategy when his dominant strategy fails, or particularly when he is feeling the strain of tension, frustration, or conflict. This can happen when his initial efforts meet nothing but resistance, or when at the point of getting down to work on a project, the subordinate's enthusiasm turns to a stubborn reluctance.

Any Grid style can be a backup to any other. For example, even a 1,9-oriented supervisor, when sharply challenged, might turn stubborn and go 9,1. Again, a boss who normally deals in a 9,9 way may meet continued resistance from a subordinate. Unable to find a way of getting on to an action basis with him, he may shift to a 5,5 approach, negotiating for some kind of compromise where both boss and subordinate will be partially satisfied.

There are no "natural" links between one particular Grid style and another in terms of dominant-to-backup. It all depends on the individual and his situation. You may sometimes see a person who habitually comes on in a 9,1 way, pressing hard, then breaking off, crestfallen. He has switched to a different set of assumptions and moved back to a 1,1 state of resignation, reacting with a sense of powerlessness, feeling that he is a victim of fate. Who knows, had he acted according to a different style from the beginning, or another set of backup assumptions, and continued talking with the subordinate, he might have gotten the reaction he wanted.

The 9,9 approach is acknowledged by supervisors as the soundest way to achieve excellent performance. This conclusion has been verified from studies throughout the U.S. and around the world. The 9,9 theory defines a model that people say with conviction they want, not only for a guide to their own conduct but also as a model of what they want their organizations and agencies to become.

PLAN OF THE BOOK

That's what the Grid is. The Grid can be used to investigate how a boss supervises in his everyday work. There are many boss-subordinate issues that can be viewed in this way. How boss and subordinate communicate is one. Another is the manner in which the boss gives work directions. Others involve managing mistakes, dealing with complaints, and how the boss reacts to hostile feelings. A final one is the matter of performance evaluation, i.e., how the boss talks with a subordinate to help him develop.

A special word needs to be said about it. One of the major approaches used today to help people develop involves having bosses interview their subordinates, usually once a year but with the option of doing so more frequently, to help each subordinate see how he's performing and how he might do better. This performance review and evaluation often involves a more or less prescribed procedure. It starts with the boss *and* (in principle) the subordinate mutually setting up performance standards and measures of results. The second step, perhaps in 6-12 months, is for the boss and subordinate to hold another session to review how well the subordinate did in meeting his performance standards. Then, whether simultaneously at annual performance rating time or not, the boss, working alone, also calibrates subordinate performance in terms of qualities such as "responsibility" and "initiative," which apply to all jobs. These evaluations are intended to be used for several purposes. One is for aiding a subordinate to see how he can improve his performance. Another is to identify special training and development opportunities. Most generally they are used as the basis for pay raises, promotions, and termination.

A boss can do any one of these things in a 9,1; 1,9; 1,1; 5,5; or 9,9 way. The next chapter describes and examines a 9,1 boss while the remaining ones examine the other Grid styles.

CHAPTER 2

9,1

By looking at Figure 1 again, you can fix in your mind where 9,1 is on the Grid. You will find it in the lower right-hand corner. It is where a 9, or high degree of concern for getting results, intersects with a 1, or a low degree of concern for people.

When a boss wants maximum production and has little concern for the thoughts, attitudes, or feelings of subordinates, he uses his authority to drive and control them. He expects them to be obedient and to cooperate. They should do whatever they are told in order to produce the wanted results. If necessary he demands "results, or else . . .!" with no ifs, ands, or buts about it.

Any boss' behavior, whether he's 9,1 or 1,1 or 1,9 or whatever, can be looked at from several different angles. Six supervisory activities that bosses carry out will be evaluated. These will aid you to see 9,1 in action.

COMMUNICATION

9,1 bosses know communication is important. Things go wrong if you don't really spell out what is expected. The 9,1 boss uses the formula, "Tell'em, tell'em you told'em, and then tell'em again." That's efficiency. There's no need then for subordinates to ask questions. Questions confuse the issue. They waste time too.

This is not to say the 9,1 boss doesn't want subordinates to communicate. He does. He wants them to nod agreement with whatever he has told them. Then there can be no doubt. They know who is going to do what, when, and how, and to report to him as soon as they are finished. Then the boss can check it and be assured everything has been done as outlined. Should his own boss want a report on a given problem he can give it without mincing words.

9,1 communication is more than just *one way*, from boss down, but it's mostly that way. The boss' primary role is to outline what's to be undertaken and how and when and by what time it should be done. The subordinate's role indicates he is going to comply and then report completion.

A 9,1 answer to the question of "Who are my subordinates?" might be "Everyone I can get to buckle under," as the following example illustrates.

• • •

One of the internal audit responsibilities in a large manufacturing company is to verify inventory from time to time. Early one morning, three audit staff members arrived unexpectedly at the Cedartown plant. They went to the front office. After identifying himself, the senior auditor said to the receptionist, "We're starting with a spot check of the Parts and Materials Store—where is it?" She replied it was located several buildings away. She offered to phone the store supervisor and ask him to send someone up to guide them there. "No need for that," the auditor said, "just sketch me a rough plan of where it is. We'll get down there. Meanwhile, don't tip off anyone we're coming."

At that moment, the factory manager buzzed the receptionist to set up a long-distance call. She informed him the auditors were outside. He came out to welcome them, saying, "Well, this is quite a surprise. We didn't expect you."

"That's the name of the game. We're not required to set up appointments in advance," the senior auditor replied curtly.

"Come on in. Let's discuss what we can do for you."

"We have our own program to work through independently here, and we're going to start right now and do it *our* way, as authorized by headquarters. Now, not to waste any more time, will you tell your girl to take us to the Parts and Materials Store?"

This was a 9,1 approach by the auditor. He commandeered the services of the factory manager's receptionist regardless of the fact that while she would be taking them to the store and returning, the telephone switchboard and her other duties would be left unattended. He was unnecessarily offensive: "Don't tip anyone off," he said, and later, in referring to her as "your girl." His remarks to the factory manager were in a similar vein.

• • •

These basic attitudes can be seen more concretely in how a boss gives directions.

GIVING DIRECTIONS

A big part of the job of a supervisor who sees himself as a 9,1 boss is to give crystal-clear directions for what he wants done. Then there can be no confusion; no excuses. If the job goes well, that is what was expected. If it isn't carried out in the right manner, the boss knows whom to blame. It's the subordinate who didn't listen or was thinking about something else, or who just didn't care enough to get the job done. So the boss gives directions in a clear-cut and direct manner. It might be better to call them orders, but no matter. He might say: "Look, Joe, a problem has arisen. I want to put you on it. Drop whatever you are doing." He then goes into detail as to what the problem is and how it should be solved. If his subordinate should ask a question the boss is likely to say, "Hold it until I've finished so you've got the full picture." When he is finishing, the boss says, "Now that's the problem. I've told you how I want it done. Don't improvise. No substitutions. No goofing off, but no shortcuts either." To seal the deal, he says, "Any questions?" Expecting none, he usually gets none. The subordinate may be too puzzled about steps 9 and 10 to notice that an essential step, 7½, was accidently left out. In any case he's beginning to forget steps 5 through 12 already. There's a feeling of despair growing, or maybe the hope that somehow he'll get through it once he starts. Yet if things go wrong, the boss can always say, "I asked you if you had any questions. You didn't have any. Your fault." It's the same when subordinates give compliance through agreement and then things go wrong as they fall through the gap where step 7½ should have been put in but was not.

● ● ●

John Epton is owner-manager of a temporary-services franchise business in Mid City. He made an early start on Monday morning, picking up the firm's mail from a downtown post office box and then going to his office. Arriving before anyone else, he ran back the telephone answering tape and began listening to customer and employee messages. He was bombarded with many minor problems that had come up during the weekend. Then the telephone rang. He caught the full blast of a customer's wrath. Her and her husband's anniversary party had been "ruined by a bunch of kids" John's firm had supplied to wait on the guests and tend bar. Not only had they turned up late but their grooming and general demeanor were "despicable." The waitresses had been ill-mannered and openly joked with one another about the "square affair." The bartender had become intoxicated during the evening and made a nuisance of himself before finally being thrown out. John absorbed the complaint, tried to apologize, and said that in view of the circumstances she would not be billed. Yet he could not placate the customer, who hung up on him after saying, "Everyone I know is going to hear about this. My husband and I are thinking of suing!" This was only the latest of several similar complaints John had received in recent weeks.

Riffling through his mail, John opened first a letter from his franchisor. It was headed "Performance Deficiencies: Standards of Dress and Service by Catering Personnel," and summarized the dissatisfied reactions of Mid City customers gathered from a nationwide mail survey by headquarters. Most were in the catering services area, where the Mid City franchise's performance fell much below the standards required under the franchise agreement. The letter ended by notifying John that a special inspection of his operation would be conducted shortly.

John began thinking back about how hard he had worked on the problems of dress and conduct over the past few months. An ever-changing pool of temporary help can never be brought up to a professional standard. He had spent much time checking them out personally, giving written guidelines, holding training sessions and so on, all the while urging cooperation and compliance. He had not been able to qualify enough reliable supervisors to cover each catering engagement, especially on weekends. At the last supervisors meeting he had strongly emphasized that they had to attain and adhere to the established efficiency standards. His urgings and various employees' promises to do better had not produced any real effect.

Upset and depressed over the bombardment of complaints and the possible adverse evaluations by the forthcoming special inspection which could mean losing his franchise, John sat down and wrote a notice to be run off and mailed to all employees that day. It stated:

> "ATTENTION ALL PERSONNEL: Your lack of self-respect in personal grooming, your tardiness and lack of courtesy when supposedly working for our customers, your lack of appreciation of the fact that for each of our customers the social event we are hired to assist represents an important occasion in their lives—all these compounded elements are dragging this business enterprise toward ruin. Effective as of now, the crew that messed up Mrs. Bruyn's party is terminated, and

so will be anyone else if I get any complaint that service wasn't the very best that a customer could have expected."

John's reaction was 9,1. The notice contained no specific explanation of what had gone wrong or what particular standards had been ignored. Its negative and abusive tone, addressed to all employees, featured threats of punishment. In coupling his published comments with an identifiable work crew, John risks being sued for libel and wrongful dismissal by those he criticized in this circular and fired so hastily.

• • •

Giving directions in a 9,1 way becomes difficult when the problem is one the boss is unfamiliar with. It is worse when neither he nor the subordinate have any very deep understanding of how to cope with the situation. The boss can't rely upon the subordinate's expertise because he can't afford to admit that he is uncertain about the best way to deal with it either. He may consult with colleagues in a sly way to get their best thinking without asking them directly what to do. Then he tells his subordinate in a direct manner what he wants done. Otherwise, he may bluff because he knows it is a rare subordinate indeed who is willing to question him. If the job gets done successfully he may never know what ingenuity and toil it took for the subordinate to get it all together. He'll say, "Good. You see—it was a breeze," and compliment himself on zipping through the problem. Beyond that, he knows that if things don't turn out well, he can pin his subordinate to the wall for being stupid, or point his finger at the Training Department for having failed to qualify his subordinates even to minimum competency standards.

These attitudes are "broadcast" day in and day out by the 9,1 boss. It comes through as an abrasive, bullying manner which someone may at any time refuse to tolerate.

• • •

The big semi-trailer had just arrived at a truck stop in Hayville on the Rocky Mountains leg of a priority long distance freight haul. Steve stayed around to check the tires and the load while his relief driver, Al Smith, went inside for a bite to eat. As he finished and was closing the cab, Steve heard a weather bulletin from the local radio station that the first winter storm was about to hit the high country. Given the expected snowfall, it would make the road over the next divide impassable within twelve hours. He hurried into the truck stop and relayed the news, which had not yet come over the Citizens Band receiver playing inside. Some crews began getting ready to move on. Others preferred to sit out the storm in Hayville as it was already getting dark.

Al, after a long wait, had just received his steak order. He was beginning to eat. Having already formed some impressions of Steve on the way up from California, he hadn't bothered to select a meal for him.

Steve came to the counter. "Hurry up, we gotta go. I'm so hungry I could eat a horse. Didn't you order for me?" Al shook his head and munched away, remarking, "Didn't know what you'd like." By now there were about eleven other truckers with rush orders in for food to go, razzing the overworked cook. Steve took in the situation and said to Al disgustedly, "Just look at that, and we've gotta get out of here quick. I'm starving and it's your fault." Al looked at him and went on eating.

"Look, we have to go. If I can't eat neither can you. Let's go!"

"You don't own the world, fella, much less my steak. Go order your meal and wait your turn!" Al replied in a quiet but tense tone of voice. Stiffening his jaw Steve directed that Al leave his steak. Others around them started to take an interest in the dispute and support Al's position. Al again refused. Finally Al said, "If you want me to go and you're big enough to do it, you can make me." There was a cheer from the entire room, followed by laughter and comments as Steve failed to meet the threat. Cursing, Steve went to the semi-trailer and waited for Al to turn up, which he did some minutes later. With Steve driving, they set off without a word to each other. Al switched to Citizen's Band, which was already broadcasting remarks of other truckdrivers who had witnessed the incident.

Back at home base, Steve went to the boss and tried to get Al fired for "being selfish and stubborn at a time when, if I hadn't gotten with it, we could have been stuck in Hayville for days. As it was, I had to drive all night over snow and ice on an empty stomach . . ." Called on the carpet, Al gave his version, the names of witnesses, and mentioned that he was ready to file a grievance if things went any further.

Steve's way of giving directions in the truck stop was 9,1 because, as driver in charge, he relied upon his rank-to-command and expected blind obedience to his wishes. He couldn't wait the fifteen minutes or so involved in ordering his own meal—hardly crucial to getting rolling again—and from then on, the consequences built up.

• • •

MANAGING MISTAKES AND ERRORS

In spite of the supervisor's best efforts at being direct and clear-cut, things do go wrong. Mistakes are made. Errors occur. People blunder. The question is, "How do 9,1 bosses deal with mistakes?"

A 9,1 boss never willingly overlooks a mistake. Why? He knows if it happens once, it will happen again and again. Regardless of precautions to avoid them, mistakes usually mean that people either were not working or that they were venting their anger by making something go wrong on purpose. He can't put up with them.

His immediate reaction on finding a mistake is "Who did it? This calls for disciplinary action." He carries out an inquisition to force the subordinate to admit his fault. This can have different kinds of results, but they all point in the same direction. It scares the subordinate so badly he becomes a bundle of nerves. Then he gets so uptight he is all thumbs; he admits doing things the wrong way even though he didn't, or he may have gotten a bum steer at the outset. Or else the subordinate becomes so resentful that every time the boss says, "You did . . . ," the subordinate says back, at least to himself, "I didn't. . . ." Out of sheer defiance he refuses to admit anything. He and the boss come to a standoff, at least on the surface. But not down deep. The reason is that this way of dealing with mistakes can result in subordinates "causing" even more mistakes. Few real perpetrators get caught. Subordinates go underground and the mistakes reappear. Those who cause them remain hidden.

• • •

Hal Coogan, the Inspection Department supervisor, was a believer in "training his own people his own way." He justified this to himself and others for several reasons.

The inspection process on finished-product items, being fairly complex, required certain theoretical background in metallurgy and electricity as well as practical knowledge of foundry work and machining, all amalgamated in what Hal termed "good judgment." Testing the finished items, identifying and tagging minor flaws that could be referred back to Production for rework, or, if necessary, rejecting the entire item which would then have to be disassembled and partly scrapped was what inspection was all about. Due to the nature of the product itself, only minor component defects could be "caught" at earlier stages of manufacture. It was at the final test inspection that any serious operating defect would become noticeable.

Thus an inspector's "go/no-go" decision was crucial either way. If he rejected an item entirely or sent it back for partial rework this would involve substantial extra cost. If he let a flawed item through and it malfunctioned in service, this could produce serious and even fatal safety hazards to users.

In Hal's judgment, local high school graduates he had hired in the past "didn't know enough" to master this inspection process without a considerable amount of coaching. College-level science graduates tended to be "too theoretical," and a strain on the budget with their higher rates of pay. They soon got bored with inspecting the same standard items day by day and often would either seek to be transferred out of the department or would quit abruptly, leaving Hal on the spot. Some time back, Hal had worked up a detailed plan for getting high-school-level trainees technically prequalified through an 18 months' period of apprenticeship spent at successive stages through manufacture and assembly. His proposals had been turned down. His policy had become one of hiring and personally training a few "sound young fellows" from high school, then gradually having them work alongside members of his dwindling group of long-term employees so as to benefit from their trade skills and years of production experience.

This week was turning out to be a "crisis week." A few days ago they had been notified that one of their installed products had exploded while in service, injuring three of the customer's employees and shutting down an important facility. With the production manager, Hal had gone to the scene to try to diagnose the cause of the malfunction. Now he was back. He knew that through some oversight in the inspection process, a faulty wiring connection had probably created the spark which touched off the explosion.

Joe Hutchins and young Maury Cole had inspected and certified that item. Hal called them into his office. "*You're* responsible, you know," he began, addressing Joe, "You're the senior tradesman. You're expected to check on every last detail, whether or not the boy's tested it."

"I'm responsible!" Joe retorted. "*You* put Maury on the job with me and said that having two of us would speed up inspection. Did you expect me to wet-nurse him and inspect everything twice as fast at the same time?"

"Hey, c'mon, what makes you think *I* blew it?" Maury interjected. "I've got better eyes and know more physics than that old goat—I *couldn't* have missed a wiring mistake like that. I remember now—I came back from the cafeteria, and he'd done most of the inspection, and he asked me to finish off and put the panels back while he took a break."

"He's making up a story as he goes along! The thing's wrecked now, isn't it?—I've seen the photographs, pieces missing, busted wires everywhere. Even the government inspectors haven't been able to show what went wrong; could have been anything. . . ."

"Shut up, the both of you, and let me think. There's going to be a court case over this—not that *I'm* worried, I didn't initial the ticket. I know one of you *must* have made a mistake, but the packers could have trouble proving it. So rest your hopes there and get back to work, and check *everything* because there's enough blood on your hands already."

"I'm not taking any more, I'm quitting!" Maury shouted, while Joe mumbled about going to see an attorney.

This was 9,1 error management by Hal. From the outset, and apparently without having brought significant facts to light, he inferred guilt on the part of others. With further inflammatory statements, he threw a scare into the two-man inspection team, which promptly blew itself apart. If the matter ends up in court with Joe and Maury as nervous and hostile witnesses taking the stand, Hal may find himself less well "covered" than he presently believes he is.

• • •

DEALING WITH COMPLAINTS

Any subordinate is going to have a complaint once in a while. Subordinates of a 9,1 boss are likely to complain—usually not directly to him at first—to ventilate their frustrations toward what they see as the boss' arrogance. Such complaints can be endless. "My equipment broke down because of poor servicing after I had requested for the fourth time that it be fixed!" "We're being pressured so hard we've all got ulcers." "We've worked so much overtime we're exhausted." Numerous other complaints are constantly brought up. The boss hears the rumbling eventually.

How does a 9,1 boss deal with complaints? His basic attitude is to see them as a lack of manliness or at least as an indication of slackness or of weakness. He either passes them off, or belittles, or bullies.

If he passes a complaint off, he says, "Here's your ticket, take it to Personnel and get it punched. . ." or "Go tell it to the chaplain. . ."or he simply puts it back on the subordinate and says, "It's a tough world for everybody." He bullies by saying, "Stop being a bleedin' heart. Buck up and be a man. Only babies cry." Or, he simply overwhelms the complainant by saying, "You've never had it so good if that's all you've got to complain about." The attitude of a 9,1 boss, in other words, is that if you listen to complaints, you are open to a never ending round of griping. You become a counseling center. Then you've got no time to get the work out. The best way to deal with complaints, in other words, is to brush them aside. Ignore them. Make the complainer ashamed of wasting your time bringing up something of such little importance.

Woe to *all* if the 9,1 boss has a hot-potato problem, which he views as a "complaint from the outside," sitting in his lap.

• • •

A scheduled punch-press production run of a large quantity of urgently needed assembly components was delayed due to problems of getting the die into proper alignment so as to cut and shape strip metal to the required tolerances. After making several adjustments and tryouts of the die when first fitting it in the press, the tool-and-die specialists had concluded that certain cutting edges were out of tolerance. They would have to be removed and replaced. Since this involved precision tool work which could not be done at the press, the fitters had removed the die and hauled it back to the tool shop where they had been working on it for the past two hours.

Meanwhile, the press stood idle. Tim Daniels, the production manager, had told his punch-press line supervisor to assign its operator to clean-up and other temporary duties, since all other presses were manned and working. On first learning the die was posing problems, Tim had proposed that the die for the next-scheduled press run be installed so production could continue while the faulty die was being put right. But Hec Wharton, the tool shop supervisor, assured him the priority-job die could be repaired and reinstalled in less time than would be involved in the next-scheduled die and materials changeover.

The factory manager had just made his morning tour, had seen the idle press, and had complained to Tim about the mounting delays and unrecoverable costs. Daniels paged Wharton again and asked what the progress was. The supervisor replied that one of his tool specialists had been working on the problem for two hours and had not had any luck in resolving it. "And where have *you* been?" Tim asked, "Why aren't *you* in the tool room supporting the tool man?" Hec answered that for the past hour-and-a-half he'd been supervising scheduled preventive maintenance work on the polishing line, and he thought his tool man could handle the die job best without his standing over him. Knowing the factory manager would be checking back soon and feeling that he had to make a decision whether or not to substitute the next-scheduled press run, Jim told the tool shop supervisor, "Go over there right now and get involved in the problem. I want a report in fifteen minutes. Get with it, or else you can think about looking for work elsewhere."

This was a 9,1 reaction. Tim Daniels, getting increasingly impatient as the die problem remained unresolved, tried to get faster results by throwing a scare into Hec Wharton. Rather than exploring with the supervisor whether or not, in fact, the tool man needed extra support to get the solution, and also considering the changeover options under present time/cost constraints, the production manager pinned blame on the supervisor, gave him an ultimatum, and rang off. He was treating the tool shop supervisor as a "problem," instead of focusing directly on getting the actual press line problem cleared up.

• • •

REACTING TO HOSTILE FEELINGS

Subordinates often get frustrated when they work day after day under a 9,1 boss. Some subordinates today are likely to tell the boss what they think. Then the 9,1 boss is into a win-lose argument or an open fight.

When people are at the beginning of a situation where they disagree over cold technical facts, discussion can be calm and the problem gets resolved. When hostile feelings are the cause of fights and win-lose arguments, though, they tend to persist and to become chronic. Every time the boss, in a gruff but conciliatory way, says, "Cool it, and let's go have a beer," the subordinate says "Get lost!" These hostile feelings crop up in a thousand different ways.

• • •

The raging influenza epidemic had severely affected River City's hot-line volunteer services and counseling center. Not only was there a sharp increase in service calls but several operators had already come down with flu. Others were feeling tired and preoccupied as they waited for their own first symptoms to show. Most telephone counselors were required to work overtime to a point where they were on nearly a seven-day work week. Increasing gaps in the ranks had to be filled by holding over counselors for two extra hours to supplement other shifts.

John Jones was already fifty minutes into extra time, had a headache, and was worried about the implications of how he felt since his wife already had the flu. This was his sixth day in a row. Feeling the need to get away from the incoming traffic for a while to have a cup of coffee, touch base with his sick wife, and unwind a little, John approached the duty team supervisor, "How long do I have to work this lousy position before I get a little relief? You spend all your time at the desk. You're unaware of what's going on. I haven't even been able to call my wife—she's down with flu too, you know—I sure could use a break."

Irritated from hearing such complaints and unable to find people to provide breaks under present traffic pressure, the supervisor, Mac Fullerton, replied hotly, "Now, see here, John —we're here to serve the community. This is a crisis situation. Quit griping. Put your mind on being professional and getting the job done."

• • •

This is a 9,1 reaction because the supervisor made no effort to resolve the telephone counselor's hostile feelings. Worse, he hadn't even explained why he could not respond to John's needs.

As already emphasized, for the 9,1 boss it is production first, and everything else next. Anything that might prevent him from getting out results is a barrier to be swept aside. Hostile feelings must be disposed of promptly. Why is this so important? Under 9,1, authority is the backbone for achieving production through people. Hostile feelings can undermine the boss' capacity for exercising his authority. Having a bad effect on production, they cannot be tolerated in the work situation. If they persist his worst fear will be realized: the system will break down.

A 9,1 boss' approach to managing hostile feelings is to try sealing them down. The fundamental rule of the 9,1 game is *suppression*. When a 9,1 boss is the target of hostile feelings, he is likely to say, "Knock it off," or "That's it, no more," or just plain, "Shut up." If that's not enough, he threatens with disciplinary action by a warning letter in the file, a day off without pay, or whatever the organization permits him to use to control challenges to his authority. Occasionally when the work is done and he can't help noticing that his subordinate is angry, he may try to clear ill feelings through an offer such as the invitation to a beer mentioned above. In the same mood a 9,1 boss might say, "You can come in half an hour late tomorrow, Millie, if you're feeling sick—I'll punch the clock for you.

However, if hostile behavior persists, the 9,1 boss arranges a transfer for the subordinate in order to get him out of his hair.

PERFORMANCE EVALUATION

A 9,1 boss sets performance standards with a subordinate by telling him what he will be expected to accomplish the next year. Once the subordinate acquiesces, then he knows what the boss demands of him for accomplishment. That is, he's *committed,* even if it's to make 10% more than possible. At the end of the period, the boss sits down and tells him how he's done. He tells him by using the measures of results set up a year before.

This performance review can be rough. Unless the subordinate has come through as a productive genius, such measures will be used to show the subordinate how far he fell short. "Failure," to a 9,1 boss is like, "You didn't get 100% on that," or "You really fell down on this one, and I can only give you 'Does Not Meet Requirements.'" The 9,1 boss, in other words, uses "negative" motivation. It's all stick and no carrot.

Maybe there'll be more frequent performance reviews—from one per year to 90-day, 60-day, or even more often—unless and until the subordinate has shaped up to meet the boss' wishes. Each time there are remarks about the Annual Rating that is drawing ever nearer. "You've really slumped this month, Jack, and it's really going to show at your next performance evaluation. Pull yourself together. Deliver from now on, will you?"

The 9,1 boss communicates that if the subordinate questions a rating, this will be taken as a challenge to the supervisor's wisdom, " . . .And I've got all the evidence, Jack—look at these *agreed* upon performance standards you didn't meet. . ."

• • •

Glen Goffman was notified to be in the conference room at 3:00 p.m. for his first annual performance evaluation wrap-up with Tony Press, the accounts supervisor. Glen arrived before his boss did. He waited, sitting casually at the table. About ten minutes after the appointed time, Tony walked in. Standing across the table from Glen, he slid the sheet across the table and said, "Here, sign this." It had been typed in final form.

Since he had transferred from another branch quite recently, this was the first performance evaluation Glen had received as a member of Tony's section. It had been one year since Glen's performance had been discussed with him by any supervisor either formally or informally. Scanning the pages, he noticed that all of Tony's check marks followed a straight line down the "satisfactory" column. As Glen well knew, "satisfactory" in the company's evaluation language was a polite way of saying "mediocre."

Glen gazed up at Tony, aghast. Tony stared back. "Would you mind, boss? I'd like to discuss this," Glen ventured for openers. The superviser remained erect and said, "There's not much to discuss. That's the way I see your performance. Of course, you're new here and that's been taken into account. Read the 'Superior' and 'Outstanding' phrases in the other columns, and you'll see where you need to make it on my team. If you have any problems I suggest you go to the Review Board, and I wish you all the luck you'll need."

This was a 9,1 approach because Tony was laying his "final judgment" on Glen and expecting him to take it calmly.

SUMMARY

The main facets of how a 9,1 supervisor operates in getting the job done are:

1. Communication tends to be one way, and mostly down. When it comes up, it is for the purpose of saluting or reporting completion.
2. Directions are given in a clear-cut and detailed way, leaving little opportunity for a subordinate to misunderstand what the supervisor wants done, and even less opportunity for him to ask questions.
3. Mistakes and errors are seen as arising from bad attitudes. Disciplinary action used is to prevent them from being repeated.
4. Complaints are a sign of weakness. The best way to handle them is to ignore them, belittle them, or overwhelm them.
5. Hostile feelings toward the supervisor are unacceptable. They lead to resistance and insubordination and cause a breakdown of the whole production system. The way to deal with them is to cut them off at the roots. Suppression is the way of pushing them back onto the subordinate. If he hasn't forgotten them tomorrow, he's malcontent and a trouble-maker.
6. Performance evaluation is a way of rewarding performers and punishing non-performers.

9,1 is a tough, authority-obedience basis of supervision. The boss imposes his will. Subordinates are tools of production. Unless they are treated as such they are sure to cause production to bog down. They are not people who should be called on to think, feel, create, or innovate. That's for supervision to do.

CHAPTER 3

1,9

The 1,9 approach is shown in the upper left corner of the Grid figure in Chapter 1. Here is where a low concern for results, 1, meets with a high concern for people, 9.

When a boss supervises in a 1,9 manner you can be certain he is highly considerate of his subordinates' thoughts and feelings. Uppermost in his mind is the hoped-for possibility that each subordinate feels good toward him. It would hurt a 1,9 supervisor, for example, if he knew that a subordinate harbored a grudge against him or that he had done anything that had turned off a subordinate.

What causes a 1,9 supervisor to have such sweetness-and-light attitudes? He believes it is good to keep any subordinate as content as possible, so that all difficulties that arise in the working day will be overcome on a pleasant basis.

To begin with, he really likes people in general and specifically the ones who work with him. In turn, he wants to be liked by them and believes that by giving his subordinates his unlimited warmth, encouragement, and support, he will maintain their loyalty. His first article of faith is that the good feelings and harmony thereby produced will guarantee that production takes care of itself. His second article of faith is that if he accepts them, they won't reject him. His fear of rejection is what makes him so eager to please.

1,9 is becoming a more common supervisory style than it was a decade ago, and it will probably increase. More of it is found in staff assignments than in line work. Within the line it is found least frequently in pressure-cooker situations. Even there there is likely to be a lot of 1,9 as a backup when pressures are off.

What is 1,9 actually like as a supervisory style?

COMMUNICATION

A 1,9-oriented boss communicates frequently with all his subordinates. He wants to assure himself that everything is okay in the sense that people are feeling good. The best way that he can do this is to stay in close, chatty conversation. Then he can detect any rumblings of unhappiness as they first begin to appear, or be helpful in assisting subordinates to adjust to their situations, or to take time to relieve whatever tensions may exist. This kind of conversation often is about topics that have nothing to do with work. And a 1,9 supervisor may like it better if he can join a friendly discussion somebody else starts rather than taking the initiative himself.

● ● ●

During a monthly Regional Headquarters supervisory sales conference, the regional manager and assistant manager were emphasizing the need for improvement in the quality of salesmen's travel vouchers. Under company procedure, area supervisors forward batches of these to regional headquarters for the office supervisor's review and the manager's approval before being sent to Accounting for payment.

Recently much time has been wasted over scrutinizing and sending back invalid vouchers. Any of these could have had embarrassing consequences for the reviewing/approval staff if they had gone through to Accounting or had been checked out by headquarters auditors. A typical error was for a salesman to claim widely varying mileages, from one week to another, for the same routine trips in his territory.

After the problem had been discussed, the regional sales manager asked his area supervisors to clear up these problems with their people. He ended, with "Remember, the office supervisor doesn't have time to re-do sloppy vouchers. If she misses any of these errors—which represent pure carelessness as far as we can see—and Marv or I sign them, all our necks could be on the line, because what would a pattern of bad vouchers look like over there, huh?"

Frank Collier, one of the area sales supervisors, went back to his unit and the following Thursday held his weekly group meeting to talk about current issues. The session began at 9:30 with refreshments and social conversation. Gradually, and in the form of gossip, Frank lightly touched on a few of the points that had been discussed in the previous week's Regional Headquarters meeting. At last he happened to recall and mention that the manager had remarked that ". . .vouchers were getting to be a problem and he asked me to say he'd appreciate it if we'd pay a little closer attention to correct completion of them."

"Nitpicking accountants again!" someone commented. Frank let the remark go by. He said, "Look, if anyone has any trouble filling these things out—recalling the mileage and so on—come see me and I'll help you with it."

• • •

This is a 1,9 approach to the problem because the supervisor did not furnish a correct rationale in terms of the accuracy of vouchers being an individual responsibility connected to proper record-keeping. He did not say that rendering flawless vouchers would spare themselves as well as the regional sales manager from being called on the carpet for irregularities detected by Accounting or auditors.

In contrast, never being too busy to communicate with a subordinate, a 1,9-oriented supervisor is always ready to discuss whatever topic is of interest to his subordinate.

All of this has the possibility of creating an easy-going, give-and-take kind of situation where production is neglected.

GIVING DIRECTIONS

When he must give directions, a 1,9-oriented supervisor is likely to mention that a problem exists but does so in a very indirect way. He hopes his subordinates will be interested enough to take the initiative themselves and ask him questions to find out more about the situation. In this way they will "own the problem." It hasn't been lowered onto them; it has been picked up by them and now it belongs to them.

In offering answers to questions the supervisor is contributing his help to their understanding of a problem that has become of concern to them. In this indirect way a 1,9 boss seems always to be helping subordinates to deal with *their* problems and almost never demanding the help of subordinates to solve a problem that he puts before them. This is all to the good when subordinates are really motivated to find and solve problems, which is unlikely under 1,9 supervision.

When it is necessary for him to ask questions of subordinates, he is likely to do so by making them very vague and general. In this way he can avoid asking "What are you working on—how are things going?" in a fashion that might annoy his subordinates or appear to be prying, prodding, or critical of their efforts. For example, rather than asking, "How much progress have you made on 'Project X'?" his preferred lead-in would be, "So you're on Project X now. Good. I know it's coming along!"

In response to the latter remark, subordinates can be as general or as specific as they wish. They are likely to feel the remark expresses confidence in them and unlikely to feel that the remark calls for more than what they're already producing.

Much of this attitude toward giving directions might be thought of as general rather than a close kind of supervision. That's what it is. It attempts to "grow" results by applying fertilizer and letting the sun shine. But the supervisor is in no position to predict whether he'll get a crop of results or a crop of weeds. It can go either way.

• • •

Dr. Sam Smith, Associate Director of the Chemical Research Center, sat at his desk reading a one-page memorandum he had just received. The document, addressed to all associate directors, was on the subject of laboratory appearance and very strongly worded. After listing several examples of slovenly housekeeping—such as cigarette butts and trash on the floor instead of in ashtrays and disposal bins—it stipulated that the appearance of the Research Center was to be meticulous from now on and it was part of an associate director's responsibilities to ensure this. Failure to comply would earn reprimand and ultimately be reflected in his annual evaluation.

Reluctantly, Sam picked up the memo and walked into his monthly administrative meeting with the Project research team supervisors. He was too worried to make light conversation. In fact, he even interrupted their coffee break to get the meeting started. Clearing his throat, he said awkwardly, "Gentlemen, I know this is a heck of a subject to bring up, but we're going to have to do more about improving the appearance of the laboratory in terms of becoming neater in regard to trash disposal and ensuring that cigarette butts end up in the ashtrays. We need to start persuading our researchers to take greater care over their housekeeping."

Several hostile remarks were immediately heard from the project supervisors, including "We aren't paid to be janitors!" Sam felt very uncomfortable. All he could manage to say was, "Well, I'd appreciate whatever can be done about keeping the areas tidy."

Later in the day when passing through the laboratory he saw that apparently no one had done anything about starting the tidiness campaign. Trying not to be noticed, he began picking up scraps of paper and cigarette butts as he moved around.

• • •

This is a 1,9 approach. When faced with rejection from his subordinates, the supervisor backed off in a fashion that almost totally de-emphasized the importance of the clean-up program. Furthermore, anticipating the "moment of truth" when the Center director would come through the door to see whether the memorandum had been complied with, he made a futile attempt at taking care of the problem himself.

Certainly this style of supervision doesn't outrage people. It doesn't tie them down with self-defeating tensions or stimulate emotions that "blow" their minds and shatter their concentrations for hours to come. It doesn't even foster personal enmity toward the supervisor. It takes a "strong" 9,1 ramrodding to do that. Under 1,9 supervision, subordinates can set whatever tempo is congenial and without fear that they will be taken to task for not producing more.

Whether or not 1,9 supervision can be successful may depend to some extent on the nature of the work being done, and to some further extent on the personal characteristics and skill level of the subordinate. For example, proud Michelangelo, at work on one of his sculptured masterpieces, wouldn't have appreciated his patron stopping by and saying, "Can't you chip any faster than that? . . . Hang on, let me check . . . no, that's not right. . . ." The feelings produced in him would make for a shaky hammer and chisel.

MANAGING MISTAKES AND ERRORS

No one likes mistakes and errors, least of all a 1,9-oriented supervisor. His heart goes out to the person who blew it, because he knows how badly that person must feel. Focusing in a warm and friendly manner on actual or imagined "hurts," rather than on the error itself, follows on the 1,9 boss assumption that people "naturally" want to do what is right. "Therefore," he reasons, "the person who has committed the error must already be feeling bad, and he'd be even more disturbed if I put emphasis on it."

Therefore, the 1,9 boss attitude toward mistakes and errors is "to accentuate the positive and eliminate the negative." He can do this by not blaming anyone. Post-mortems don't help. Instead, he cushions the subordinate in some manner such as, "Well, I know you did your best. Don't worry, things will work out. We'll look after it." The blame is not placed upon the subordinate and he is helped to find relief from any blame he may be feeling from within. If that doesn't work, the 1,9 boss is likely to coddle the troubled subordinate and encourage him that all is "forgiven and forgotten." This attitude is particularly evident when the mistake or error has been one of violating rules or policies. Under a 1,9 attitude policies and procedures are not "rigid fences that you force people to stay within." They are guideline indicators rather than fixed or rigid requirements. "After all, when someone's upset and confused, it's awfully diffi-cult to walk the line." Looking at it from this angle, the 1,9 boss sees no need to be constantly vigilant for a mistake or error. By the same token, even if a subordinate does go against important rules or regulations the 1,9 attitude is that a gentle reminder and another chance will really help the person to realize and avoid the problem again, and appreciate the boss all the more for not getting nasty.

• • •

Bill Robertson, workshop supervisor in a boat-building firm, was walking across the shop to the front office one morning when he saw Chuck Davis, one of his carpenters, pick up a piece of plywood and smash it violently down upon a bandsaw, shat-tering the piece of wood and breaking the bandsaw blade. Bill immediately rushed over to see what the problem was. Chuck's face was red and he seemed very upset about something.

"What's wrong, Chuck?" Bill asked. The carpenter said, "Aw, I can't cut anything right today. Everything I try to saw turns out wrong, won't fit. . . ." Interrupting, Bill said, "No, I don't mean about work—how are you feeling, Chuck? You seem so upset. Is something at home bothering you?" Chuck, calmer now, yawned and stretched. "No, I went out with the boys last night and got home a little late, y'know, around 3:30. I guess I'm just tired today."

"Well, why don't you take a break, go have a cup of coffee. Relax awhile, and you'll feel better."

"Thanks, I'll do that." Chuck grinned, and remarked, "You're a real pal, not like some boses I used to have. I like it here, Bill, you can count on me to stay." He went off to the cafeteria.

Bill felt great. This was the best compliment he'd received in quite a while. The next half hour was pure pleasure as he stayed to fix Chuck's bandsaw and tidy the workplace so that his subordinate could get off to a good start whenever he returned.

• • •

It was a 1,9 approach in that the supervisor's major concern was for the welfare of the employee, with little or no concern for productivity of the shop, the proper use of equipment and materials, or self-responsibility by the employee being fit for the job.

A 1,9 boss feels that "harsh" attitudes toward mistakes and errors can hurt a good relationship. Rather, his own view is that a boss should be generous in understanding what has happened, sympathetic with "victims" of the tragedy, and helpful in clearing up the after effects of whatever subordinates did. To him, mistakes and errors are like sand in the wheels of progress. Unless handled in the way described, they can produce friction, disrupt harmony, and chill the kind of warmth and harmony that boss and subordinates have a right to enjoy in their interactions with one another.

DEALING WITH COMPLAINTS

When a 1,9 boss hears complaints from subordinates, these will likely be worrisome to him, the more so if the complaints are personal.

Complaints about the situation, or about the equipment, or about the inevitable pressure the system creates are not so distressing because the 1,9 boss realizes that subordinates don't expect him to be able to wave a wand and eliminate these sources of irritation. In responding to such complaints, the 1,9 boss can join in and agree with the complaint being expressed. This tells the subordinate the boss is with him as fellow sufferer. It relieves the boss because the complaint does not create a distance between them.

However, the situation is different when the complaint is personal and in the sense of involving something the boss should have done and didn't do, or did and shouldn't have. The 1,9 boss takes the complaint at face value. He is likely to react with horror to something which might be seen by others more objectively as no more than a tempest in a teapot. When faced with such a situation, a 1,9 boss does whatever is within his ability in order to ease disturbed feelings. That might be an apology; it might be to promise it won't happen again; it might involve doing some kind of unexpected favor for the subordinate. In this way the boss can avoid rejection by letting the subordinate know he's sorry and "Let's have no hard feelings." These steps can take the sting out of any antagonism the subordinate may have felt and replace it with a sense of harmony.

• • •

In a certain hospital, the emergency room staff works straight eight-hour shifts with no provision for a lunch period as such. Depending upon the casualty intake position at any given moment a doctor, nurse, or orderly is permitted to eat outside the emergency room facilities provided he is immediately available if needed. For this purpose a room with coffee and food-warming equipment is available a few steps away. But the hospital cafeteria is considered too far away from the emergency room for personnel to be recalled with the speed required.

During one of the monthly staff meetings, one of the registered nurses, Terry McLaren, mentioned she was becoming disenchanted with having to bring lunch from home. Others offered the same complaint. Toward the end of the meeting, several pressed for a ruling from Dr. Grant on whether or not they could go to the cafeteria one at a time to eat, with the understanding that they'd hurry back as soon as paged. At a fast clip, this would take about three minutes.

"Well, it's very unfortunate that the cafeteria isn't more conveniently near," Dr. Grant responded. "But we *do* have a microwave oven in the break room—don't you find it's nice to bring food from home and warm it up here?"

"Well, some might, but with a husband and children I wouldn't, and it's the same for others too," Terry rejoined.

There were murmurs of agreement. Dr. Grant looked ill at ease. "Well, I'm sure that's the case. Personally, all I can say is that I always buy a sandwich or something in the little shop across the street before coming on duty, and I find their food quite tasty."

Several staff members reacted by saying they couldn't agree with Dr. Grant's opinion that the sandwich shop food was decent. In fact, it was known as "ptomaine pit," its prices were steep, and so on. As for bringing lunches: many of the male staff members' wives had jobs as well as children, and thus found it inconvenient to prepare food at home. Dr. Grant, obviously uncomfortable, said, "Well, I suppose it would be alright if you only went one at a time for a snack in the cafeteria, but please hurry back the moment you're paged."

• • •

This response was 1,9 because even though the standards were well defined by emergency room policy and procedures, the chief, rather than to risk becoming unpopular with these nurses and orderlies, surrendered and took the most comfortable position on the issue.

REACTING TO HOSTILE FEELINGS

A 1,9 boss shatters in the face of hostile feelings even more than when faced with complaints. The reasons seem to be that hostile feelings are only a few degrees removed from active dislike, and active dislike is only a step or two away from hate. For a 1,9-oriented person this path seems to lead to disaster because it gets into undermining the very foundations of the main security that he has—that which comes from being in a warm and friendly relationship with other people. Hostility, conflict, antagonism—these are all emotions that a 1,9 person will do his utmost to avoid. This means a 1,9 boss simply does not try to face up to hostile feelings. He seeks ways to smooth over these kinds of negative feelings if they come up. The continued focus of his efforts, of course, is to try to ensure that they're not generated at all.

There are many ways a 1,9 supervisor can attempt to reestablish harmony. People can be cajoled and coaxed into looking at how good things are relative to how bad they might be. "It's a dog's life, Wilbur, and like yourself I can hardly stand it at times, but after all, we've got job security." In this way he can get people to pay attention to what's positive and to turn their minds away from the negatives that are having a tension-producing effect. The mental attitude seems to be "every cloud has a silver lining" or "every day in every way we are getting better and better."

This kind of warm, generous acceptance of the person who is feeling hostile, even though it doesn't focus on the hostility itself, can often turn the situation around with harmony replacing the hostility previously felt. This is partly so because when the 1,9-oriented boss reacts in this "hurt" manner, wanting to make amends and get back into a warm relationship, it is very difficult for a hostile subordinate to maintain his hostility. He is more likely to say, "Ah, let's forget it," and move on to another topic or matter where good feelings can be restored.

• • •

Paul Smith, a technician working for a contractor firm, braked the pickup truck to a halt directly in front of the Service Building main entrance, double-parked, turned on the emergency flasher, and dashed into the building to pick up several components he needed to repair an engine generator. He was only gone about 7 or 8 minutes, but as he returned lugging the heavy equipment he noticed a police car pulling away from the area.

Paul loaded his equipment and jumped in the front seat to have his vision blocked by a piece of paper stuck in the windshield wiper. He got out and saw he had a traffic ticket for double parking. Physically very uncomfortable due to carrying the heavy equipment as well as experiencing the heat of the cab on this summer day, he ripped the ticket off the windshield, sped back to his firm's workshop, and dashed into his foreman's office. He slammed the ticket on Gene Foley's desk and burst out, "Those stupid cops are harrassing us—look at this—I just got a ticket for double parking while I was busting myself carrying out generator components!" Gene, rather bewildered by the sudden attack, said, "Gee, Paul, I'm sorry about that. I can see why it makes you feel bad. It's so undeserved. I can hardly believe the police would give one of us a ticket. I'm going to have to take this to the boss and see what can be done about it. Meanwhile, why don't you take a break."

• • •

This is a 1,9 response by the supervisor in that he had no concern for the fact—if he'd found out about it—that Paul had double parked the truck, almost blocking a narrow driveway. Instead he tried to comfort the employee and apologize for the annoying actions of others.

PERFORMANCE EVALUATION

For a 1,9 supervisor, performance evaluation can be like driving down a road that has been land-mined. The reason is his fear that any remark, no matter how well intended, may be taken by his subordinate as a criticism or as a sign of the subordinate's weakness. When this is so, if the subordinate reacts defensively, the 1,9 boss is in trouble. He now must back up what he has said, or else suffer the embarrassment of retraction.

For these reasons a 1,9 boss deals very gingerly with performance evaluation. His goal, of course, is to keep things on the positive side. He is likely to operate on the proposition that people improve by putting additional effort on strengthening their skills rather than trying to eliminate defects. In this way, he can talk with subordinates about what their positive capabilities are and is relieved from any need to talk about defects or deficiencies. This means the conversation can be a positive one because each identified skill he points out to a subordinate is equivalent with paying a compliment. Since deficiencies don't have to be mentioned, the 1,9 boss is not placed in what would be an untenable position—that of pointing to deficiencies which, from his angle, are equivalent to presenting a criticism.

Mary McCarthy, chief of the payroll section in Accounts, walked out of her office. She approached Betty Klein, one of the clerks. She handed Betty a form, gently explaining to her the performance evaluation report was due and that, since Betty was also in line for a pay increase, ". . .this would be a real good time to get it filled out." Betty scanned the form, looked up and said, "Well, Mary—there's nothing on it!" Mary replied, "Well, you know, Betty, it would look like Judgment Day if I'd checked off this thing in advance. Why don't you go ahead and fill it out as you view your performance."

Betty was somewhat taken aback by this because she was uncomfortable with having, in effect, to evaluate herself. She also felt disappointed that her boss didn't place enough importance upon her performance to even bother to evaluate it. She said to Mary, "I would rather that *you* fill it out." Mary responded, "I just want to do whatever is fair to you, so why don't you fill it out and if I see anything I think is unreasonable, I'll talk with you about it." Upon reaching this agreement, Mary left, saying, "Any time you're finished, drop it in the tray, okay?"

• • •

This is a 1,9 approach to a performance evaluation because the supervisor has an overwhelming concern for neither hurting personal feelings nor disappointing the employee about her performance.

SUMMARY

The 1,9 style of supervision emphasizes the overriding importance of good relations. Its thesis is that if subordinates are happy, contented, and feel a sense of warmth and self-worth and acceptance, they will then want to cooperate with the system. Here's how a 1,9 supervisor thinks about key elements of supervision.

1. Communications are seen by a 1,9 supervisor as at the very heart of good relationships. If boss and subordinate are able to talk freely and informally and with feelings of mutual

sharing, then almost everything else, it can be hoped, will be all right. 1,9 bosses, then, are prepared to talk about whatever subordinates want to talk about. It doesn't need to be work related. Any topic will do because it provides an opportunity for two people to share their thoughts and feelings and emotions in a mutually appreciative way.

2. Directions are offered in a general fashion, always with the anticipation and hope that subordinates will begin asking questions. And as they do, they will feel "ownership" of the problem. Then the boss can respond to questions in a way that makes it possible for him to be helpful and constructive to the subordinates who feel the need for this kind of assistance.

3. Mistakes and errors by subordinates are something that a 1,9 boss feels are best dealt with by not tackling them as problems. Believing subordinates get unhappy with themselves for having made a mistake or committed an error, the better approach to dealing with subordinates under these conditions is to give them understanding, support, and forgiveness.

4. Complaints by subordinates which relate to work, or to the system, or to the equipment—things about which the boss cannot be expected to do too much—are likely to be dealt with by the boss agreeing with subordinates that the situation is unfortunate or just too bad. If their complaints are about the boss himself, the matter is viewed as serious indeed. A 1,9 boss under these conditions is likely to try to shift attention away from himself by getting people to agree that "every cloud has a silver lining," or in some other way smooth over the difference and get people to be nice to one another.

5. Hostile feelings expressed against the boss are devastating to him. They make him want to apologize, if that is appropriate, or to make amends if that will help to restore good relations.

6. Periodic performance evaluation chores are best done in this way. A 1,9 boss makes the assumption you can help people much more by emphasizing their strengths and assisting them to improve what they already do well, rather than harping on deficiencies they can do very little about correcting anyway. Thus, a 1,9 boss conducts a performance evaluation in a manner that causes his subordinates to feel complimented rather than criticized.

CHAPTER 4

1,1

The 1,1 supervisory style is where 1, a low concern for results, joins together with 1, a low concern for people. It's in the
lower left corner of Figure 1, on page 5. It's the "see no evil,
hear no evil, speak no evil" approach. The secret of a successful 1,1 is to be visible without being seen; to be present without
being noticed. You are visible—part of the background and apparently going through your paces—and yet not seen because
you do nothing to draw your colleagues' attention to your pres-
ence. You are present but unnoticed. Then you're out of the
firing line of anyone who could take action against you. They
have no occasion to. You've done nothing wrong. You have em-
barassed no one. You've not gotten in anyone's way. You've not
been a troublemaker. The fact you don't do anything much of
a constructive character isn't particularly noticed. What's more,
you have done enough to avoid being labeled a shirker or a
free-loader—good attendance record, always behind your desk.
As far as anyone else knows, you do have some concern for
production.

The fact is, a supervisor *can* be a 1, 1 supervisor and even
make progress up the ladder. The reason is that, seniority being
what it is, a person keeps floating up in annual income incre-
ments and even in rank. After all, the higher up the ladder you
get, the more scope for delegation. "You know what the President wants, Miller, so I'm giving you full authority to accom-

plish this. You're a promising young fellow, and this project will test what you can do." So he's even a "developer," in his fashion.

We need to understand 1,1 as a supervisory style. One reason is that this approach is quite common. Another is that the 1,1 approach can slow organization performance down to a snail's pace without anyone being able to "spot" why.

COMMUNICATION

There are a number of ways a 1,1 boss goes about communicating. There is little need for him to converse since he does not think in terms of what information he needs to give a subordinate. For example, he is unlikely to pose questions to subordinates. Questions provoke answers and sometimes counter-questions, and then he would have to deal with them. Rather, he is likely to leave it up to the subordinate to ask questions on the assumption the subordinate is supposed to know what he needs to know. The 1,1 boss says to himself, "If he wants the information, he'll ask for it." If he does, the boss answers it if he knows how, and he can promise to find out if he doesn't. More easily, "Frank's the expert on that—why don't you go see him?"

When it comes to listening, a 1,1 supervisor is not too attentive. This kind of a boss is neither emotionally involved with his subordinate's problems, nor does he wear his own ego on his shirt, needing to demonstrate his knowledge in solving his subordinates' problems. He lets subordinates talk as much as they wish, but tunes himself out and thinks about other things. If a remark is made again or a question repeated, he can always say, "Oh, sorry, I didn't get what you said." One result of this kind of attitude toward communication is that a 1,1 boss is likely to be thought of as "quiet, thoughtful—he really mulls over a problem, never talks off the top of his head." He might even get a plaudit for concentrating on his own problems so hard he does not hear the outside world. One of the great advantages of this is that others frequently avoid interrupting the quiet person who seems busily engaged in some activity, even though from the 1,1 person's angle he knows he's thinking about duck hunting or some other topic. If agreement is what is wanted, he can nod or shake his head, whichever way the subordinate wants it. If he gets pushed for an answer, he can double-talk his way around, telling the subordinate in unspecific terms what might be done. He can thus avoid the criticism that otherwise might be his were the subordinate's performance to turn out badly. "Obviously, sir, I could hardly imagine that Miller would go the way he did on the project. You see, I showed him your clear general guidelines. . . ."

• • •

Bill Legge, the personnel officer at East Wickham, called head office and informed the Personnel Division there that the local maintenance foreman, Joe Hillman, was not performing his functions properly because, it was suspected, of taking many unauthorized absences during working hours. This information had been passed to Bill by Jeff Stokes, the maintenance chief, with the request, "Cut through the rigamarole somehow and help me get him fired." Rather than quote Stokes verbatim, Bill interpreted to headquarters, "Joe disappears for an hour or two here, two hours there. It's impossible to find him anywhere, but he comes back and says he was working somewhere else. It's very hard to pin him down." He asked for advice as to his course of action, and was told he and Joe's boss should document the performance situation, double-check the time records, and build a case for termination if one was warranted.

At a later date, headquarters received a "Confidential-Urgent" letter from Joe Hillman. He said the he was doing his job effectively around a wide territory and that the real problem was with his boss, Stokes, who had a personal grudge against him that stemmed from an off-the-job incident. Independent investigation by headquarters revealed that, in fact, Joe was right. The chief had been collecting a stack of maintenance request-for-authorization forms and job-time records, as well as materials vouchers that required payment and should have been processed. These had all been prepared by Joe in a prompt and orderly way but were being held under the guise of collecting evidence and "building" a case of incompetency against Joe. This was being done with the full knowledge of the Personnel Officer who did nothing. Joe was not initially aware of what was happening and no action had been officially taken against him. It was when Joe caught flak from an unpaid supplier, tracked down the records in the office and found them bundled up in a "Joe file" with a draft case-for-termination memorandum, that he called headquarters.

• • •

This illustrates a 1,1 approach on the part of the local Personnel Officer. He did not bother to exercise his responsibilities to find out whether or not Stokes' allegations were factually based. If he had done so, he would have found action was evidently needed in the case of Stokes rather than Hillman. But instead, Bill's 1,1 attitude brought him into collusion with Stokes; preventing, as it did for awhile, some pertinent information from being communicated.

GIVING DIRECTIONS

The supervisory approach to giving directions under 1,1 often would be to say, "Here's what they want done. It's set out in this memo. Let me know when you're finished." Then he leaves people alone. He lets them do their work as they see fit, hoping they will solve their problems by getting help from one another rather than coming back for his assistance.

The 1,1-oriented supervisor doesn't think in terms of goals or schedules. Because he turns the problem over to his subordinates, he himself does little planning.

• • •

Stan Fletcher, district foreman of a state-wide wrecker service, walked into the District Manager's office, inspired by a problem and what he was seeing as an excellent solution to it.

Stan believed that their Rosedale district, one of the largest and most mountainous areas in the state, desperately needed to take action through the budgetary process to obtain a more powerful two-way radio communication system in order to keep in better touch with wrecker vehicles and dispatch them more efficiently. Logan Burr, the manager, responded, "Well, I don't see anything wrong with the level of service we've been giving. I haven't had many complaints about it. And you know what a tight-fisted bunch they are at head office. The budget process is complicated. It's going to take a lot of work on our part, and there's little hope of our getting the equipment. And besides, we're pretty short-handed right now." Stan continued to argue persuasively. He provided examples and reasons why it would be beneficial to make the effort. The district manager, deadpan, let him talk on for a while and then said, "Well, you'd better get back to work. I'll see what I can do about it." Stan left, and Logan turned back to reading the latest sports magazine until five o'clock rolled around.

A week later Stan approached the district manager. He inquired about what he had been able to do regarding the improved radio communication system they had discussed. Logan solemnly replied he had been thinking about it and intended to look into the budgetary process required to bring the item to head office's attention. "Well, I won't keep you, Stan. Thanks for bringing it up." He was gone.

• • •

This is a 1,1 approach. The district manager failed to respond candidly to Fletcher's request. It should be obvious to Fletcher as well as the reader that the Chief really intended to do nothing.

In that sense, you might call the 1,1 supervisor a message carrier. He takes the word from the level above and hands it to one level below, putting as little extra on it as possible. This is passing directions "through proper channels" by becoming part of the pipeline itself.

MANAGING MISTAKES AND ERRORS

A 1,1 boss knows how to "not see" a mistake or an error. He more or less ignores them on a "see no mistakes . . ." basis. The only time he might get stirred up about a mistake or an error is when he knows that if the mistake will be known above him he'll catch it. To avoid trouble as much as possible, though, he places responsibility in such a way as to relieve himself from being accountable.

● ● ●

Sam Young, an installation supervisor with Browne Security Systems, shuffled slowly toward his boss' office, revolving in his mind a situation that had occurred a couple of hours ago in a customer's residence. He and his assistant had been about to lift a valuable painting from the wall to install an alarm device behind it when his assistant lost his grip. The painting thudded to the floor, scratching the wall as it fell. The frame had a small crack at its corner, and to make matters worse, there was a deep indentation in the molding at the foot of the wall. The customer was out at the time. After a few seconds of panic, Sam came to his senses and began thinking what to do. This was a recently completed house by a well-known builder. Hoping his guess was right, Sam hurried to the garage where, sure enough, he found the builder's paint cans and wallpaper remnants. Sam also had a kit of equipment and materials out front in his truck. Having organized these he sent his assistant out to stand watch and warn him if the customer suddenly returned. Sam set to work with spackling compound, razor blade, glue, paint and stain. Within an hour he had patched and touched up the frame, wall, and molding so that all looked as good as new. After running the air conditioner full blast to clear away the paint smell while they completed the alarm installation and tidied up, Sam had checked one final time to ensure that traces of the disaster were completely disguised before they left.

Sam walked into his boss' office and remarked, "We had a

little accident out at Mrs. Taylor's this afternoon. She was out at the time, fortunately. That clumsy Thompson you put on my crew dropped something and it scraped one of her walls. . . ."

"Mrs. Taylor's? Good grief, that's all we need!"

"Don't worry—I found the builder's materials out back and touched up everything to perfection. Chances are she'll never notice a thing, but if she smells paint or sees a little hairline in the wallpaper where I replaced the part that had been scratched, you can mention the secret wiring and what all we had to do to protect her valuables."

"Okay—you're sure that's all?"

"Yep."

"And what about Thompson—think we ought to fire him?"

"No, he got the scare of his life and he'll be more careful in the future. He's learned some tricks of the touch-up trade, too, and that's what's needed in this business at times."

• • •

The installation supervisor's approach to the situation was 1,1 because rather than being frank with the customer and his boss after the accident, he invested energy and guile in a "cover-up" to cover himself. In regard to his assistant, he is proceeding on a "less said, the better" basis rather than training the man in installation-related skills that seem to be lacking at present.

The 1,1 supervisor tries to set up, in advance, excuses for self-protection so that he won't get tagged for the big ones that are detected and might otherwise make his employment insecure. He may say, "Oh, there's no way to train good workers any more. They're the new generation (or lacking in experience, or poorly trained, or poorly selected, or poorly paid). What can I do?" The 1,1 attitude is that mistakes are more or less inevitable. ". . . Since you can't do much about them, why worry your head off?"

DEALING WITH COMPLAINTS

The 1,1 supervisor steers his relationships with subordinates along a complaint-free path. He avoids being open to subordinates' complaints and yet they couldn't describe him as ignoring them either. The easiest way for him to avoid getting involved is not to get drawn into someone else's problems. Once a complaint is raised his strategy may be to acknowledge it with a brief "Hmm, that's bad," comment to imply that he'll be giving it further thought. Then, for all practical purposes, he ignores it. Or he might respond with "Yes, I know. That's one of the big hangups around here. But they soon tag you as a troublemaker if you try to do anything about it." Thus he implies that he goes along with it, for what that's worth. His neutrality makes it possible to live in a world where he sees no disagreement, hears no disagreement, and speaks no disagreement. It's the smooth surface of a deep-lying apathy others are likely to become aware of as time passes. "Why tell him? What's the use? He wouldn't understand." They might say, with greater generosity, "He understands, but he wouldn't be able to do much about it."

● ● ●

In a rural power and light company, it became necessary to involve electronics technicians in work normally carried out by maintenance specialists with lesser skills. This was due to a shortage of tradesmen who specialized in refrigeration, air conditioning, and engine generator type work.

Until such time as an additional tradesman could be recruited for Smithville Power and Light, the ongoing problem was that part of the routine maintenance work was not presently being accomplished. In response, particularly to customer complaints from outlying areas, an executive decision was made that it would be necessary for electronics technicians, while visiting their sites for maintenance, to do some of the customer service work such as fixing refrigerators, air conditioners, motors, and so on.

When Tom Egan, technical supervisor, convened a meeting to announce this decision, he began by saying that it was now company policy that they do customer maintenance work around the local area whenever visiting their facilities. The technicians, particularly Bert Hughes, did not agree with this policy. Bert was very vocal, saying in terms of his job description that he was not required to do lesser skill type work such as repairing some farmer's electric tools or a washing machine. Tom replied, "This is the policy. There's nothing I can do about it. I've got no control over it."

• • •

This was a 1,1 supervisory response because Tom was merely passing down policy information without explaining the rationale behind the requirement.

Sometimes a subordinate might try to get his 1,1 supervisor to do something specific about a complaint. He persists even after the boss has said he's sorry but it's something he can do nothing about. Maybe the subordinate has begun to talk about going up through grievance channels, so the boss begins to feel uncomfortable. Then he might shift the conversation by indicating he will consult up the organization to get the answer. After a while, having gotten no answer, the subordinate may put the question as to what he found out.

Then the boss probably replies with vague remarks like, "There doesn't seem to be a policy on that," or "They couldn't decide, so I guess they're going to take it upstairs."

If the subordinate continues to press his complaint and asks what to do, his 1,1 supervisor is likely to say, "It's up to you," or "I wouldn't want to influence your decision," or "Well, you're going to have to fill out a lot of forms, so go see so-and-so," or "There are all kinds of pros and cons, and I'm not an expert." Another typical 1,1 response in a down-to-the-wire situation is, "Well, there are two ways you might go about it, but you probably will have a better feel than I for which is best."

In these various ways, characteristics of the 1,1 supervisor come to the fore. He is not closed. He is not antagonistic. He is not open. He is not warm. He is not cold. He is not responsive. He is not negative. So what **is** he? The best answer is that he is bland, soggy, opaque, plastic. You might think he's one of those store-window figures wired for sound and transferred to your organization, and yet you know that he must somehow be alive because he breathes and moves. He arrives, and leaves. He even seems to take part in the organization's life.

REACTIONS TO HOSTILE FEELINGS

A 1,1 boss reacts to hostile feelings by not acting as a boss. Since he has no intention of being drawn in, he can keep his cool. Getting a polite but poker face reaction or no reply at all, the subordinate is likely to say, either aloud or to himself, "Aw, to heck with it," and walk away.

Some 1,1-oriented supervisors wear down their subordinates' hostile feelings much in the same way as a skillful angler plays a fish till it's played out. The boss might listen silently to his subordinate's tirade. Whenever the subordinate ceases, he waits. He might even be skillful enough to act like he was about to interrupt the subordinate in order to answer but quickly yields the floor when the subordinate starts up again. In this way he prompts the subordinate, time and time again, to vent his anger until eventually the subordinate has nothing more to say. No harm has been done. They might even walk away together.

● ● ●

Data processing supervisors, computer programmers and operators are very sensitive in regard to the qualities and functioning of the equipment. The EDP technician is expected to keep the system in peak performance. The data processing supervisor, programmer or operator, when his system is in optimum condition, is completely happy with it. But he rarely has the time or the thought to compliment the EDP technician. However, whenever he detects the system deteriorating or if it suddenly goes down completely, he is still in the crucial business of having, say, to supervise a management information system along with payroll and whatever other programs are currently being run. With lightning speed and supercharged emotions they get on the phone to the EDP technician.

From where he is, the technician hears only the things that are said when his system is down. He seldom knows about the good things when, helped by his careful attention, the EDP system performs at peak for extended periods. Eventually this gets to him. He goes to his own supervisor to discuss it.

Clark Higgs, totally frustrated by the end of an extra-busy shift, went to Steve Colby and sounded off loud and long. The supervisor sat back and listened. Then he said, "Oh, don't worry about it, don't pay any attention to those operators, it's just the way they are. They've just got to complain about something. What could anyone do about it anyway?"

• • •

This is 1,1 because the supervisor had clearly adopted a "do nothing" attitude and would offer no constructive comments, far less propose doing anything about getting better rapport with the data processing supervisor and his people.

• • •

Clyde Millspaugh, an Engineering Division supervisor, approached his secretary and asked her to retype a few pages because the technician's name on the position description had changed. Wanda responded belligerently with, "We don't retype position descriptions just for that." Clyde mumbled, "The Chief said we should do it," and walked off.

Wanda glared at his retreating back and muttered something. She did not retype the sheets. Instead, she called Personnel Division and asked them if it was necessary to retype just to change the name of the supervisor. The Personnel man said as far as he was concerned, it wasn't necessary. Wanda then strode into Clyde's office to pass on Personnel's opinion. "So you *see*, Mister Millspaugh, I was *right*—there's no need to retype it." Her supervisor, hardly looking up, said, "Okay, if Personnel says so."

This was a 1,1 approach because the supervisor took no account of the employee's hostile feelings. Furthermore, he had initially failed to provide sufficient background information about why he wanted a retype.

It's quicker to describe a 1,1 boss' way of reacting to hostile feelings by telling what it is *not*. He doesn't seek on his own initiative to become aware of hostile feelings that may bear on him. He doesn't run away from them. He doesn't ignore them when they are expressed. He doesn't respond to them. He doesn't get uptight, but he doesn't brush them off as trivial. In a certain sense he accepts the expressions of hostile feelings like the walls of a soundproof room. Yet the subordinate who speaks them, if he notices closely what is going on, gains little satisfaction from having expressed his hostile emotions to the boss. On the other hand he, the subordinate, doesn't get punished or criticized. Yet he knows deep down that having made the effort didn't change much. The same old situation will be around tomorrow, the next day, and next year.

PERFORMANCE REVIEW AND EVALUATION

If he has the option of holding performance review interviews at longer or shorter intervals, the 1,1 supervisor goes to the upper limit—say, once a year. The interview itself won't take long. "Well, here we go again, Smathers, another of these routines we have to go through for some reason. . . ."

Performance appraisal reports create few problems. The 1,1-oriented boss' preferred approach is to treat everyone about equal.

• • •

Horace Venn, a buyer at Treecey's Department Store, suddenly reminded at 8:30 a.m. by telephone that Sam Gibbs was due a performance rating a couple of days ago, hurriedly filled out the appraisal form. He went to the Men's Shop and approached Sam, who was doing a merchandise check and rearrangement and had suits, shirts and ties spread all over the counters and fixtures. Horace said, "Why don't you take a break and come into the office; I want to talk to you about your Performance Rating." Once in the office, he handed the rating form to Sam. It reflected "Satisfactory" performance in all parts.

Sam, unprepared to discuss a year's performance off the top of his head, and not having had any progress interviews during the previous twelve months, was taken aback. Rather weakly he said, "My rating last year was a lot better than that." Horace replied, "Well, as you're aware, the rating system's been revised throughout the store, resulting in what seem to be lower ratings." Sam still was not satisfied and became more and more upset about the situation. He said, "That may be true, but I certainly think my performance deserves more discussion and a better rating than this." Horace responded, "Well, as you see, they had the satisfactory column outlined in heavy ink, and that's where eighty percent of us are supposed to be. Why, they even put me there." Looking at his watch, the buyer said, "Look, it's almost opening time. You had better get that merchandise put back together before the doors open. If you want to talk about this further, the form tells you who you can see."

• • •

This was a 1,1 approach because Horace obviously took scant interest either in whether the rating he had produced was an objective appraisal of Sam's past year's performance or the feelings Sam had about the rating. Yet he had tried to let Sam get the impression that "everyone's treated alike." In this way he is not often called upon to explain or justify distinctions drawn between his subordinates. As a bonus benefit, he might build a reputation of being "fair." If called upon to write an evaluative description, he learned long ago how to write these in ways that make them acceptable without their having much communication value. He does this by keeping his remarks vague, abstract, and provisional, often implying a positive attitude but rarely being specific. His bosses can put just about whatever interpretation *they* want on it.

SUMMARY

A 1,1 supervisor stays on the job in order to go on to retirement. In fact, by the time he's gotten things squared away, in effect he's already converted his salary into a pension. The name of the game is "coast." He doesn't find it difficult to be visible and looking occupied without being seen or being productive. He contributes as little as possible without getting himself in trouble. His basic approach can be summarized in the following way:

1. Communication tends to be on a message-passing basis. He tells others what he has been told and reports whatever the next level higher requests. "You asked for this and they did that."

2. Directions are given in a general way. Subordinates are left on their own initiative to figure the best way to carry out whatever assignments they have been given.

3. Mistakes and errors are inevitable and the best way *not* to get in trouble about them is not to see them.

4. The way a 1,1 supervisor deals with his subordinates may or may not cause them to be complainers. He does not go around hunting for complaints yet he does "hear" when complaints are expressed. But he "hears" in a special way. The likelihood is that after a while the person doing the complaining will drop it anyway. But if he doesn't, the 1,1-oriented supervisor can indicate he has passed the problem up to the next level for reaction. He hasn't heard back yet what they think should be done.

5. When reacting to hostile feelings, a 1,1 supervisor doesn't try to avoid listening by escaping from the situation, or hiding. On the other hand he doesn't feel personally involved when hostile feelings are expressed. His policy is that if you listen without reacting, pretty soon the person with the hostile feelings will get them out of his system. That will be the end of it. Or he just lets the complainer wear himself out.

6. Performance review and evaluation are easy for a 1,1 supervisor. He has low standards for what he expects of others. Objective-setting with the subordinate is tackled reluctantly and he conducts this and the prescribed followup interviewing in a very superficial manner. Therefore, he can accept whatever performances they turn in almost without regard for the contribution they make.

You might think 1,1 supervisors are rare birds indeed. Yet they are found at executive, managerial, and supervisory levels from the top to the bottom. They are difficult to see. This is because they have learned the act of blending into the woodwork in such a manner as to be a piece of the furniture. Problems pass them by without it being noticed that they made little or no contribution to solving them.

CHAPTER 5

5,5

The 5,5 theory of supervision is identified in the middle of the Grid in Figure 1. In this case, a moderate degree of concern for production or results is combined with a moderate degree of concern for the people being supervised. This is the most common theory of supervision today. Its popularity is growing. As 9,1 comes to be more unacceptable, many supervisors know nothing else better to do than to shift into a 5,5 orientation.

You can get a sense of what 5,5 is all about by examining some well-known phrases. "A half loaf is better than none" is one kind of 5,5 attitude. Another is "To get along you've got to go along." A third is "You scratch my back and I'll scratch yours." A common attitude underlies each of these. The attitude is that while you don't go all the way to 9 on either of the Grid dimensions, you don't take up the "couldn't care less" attitude either, because this is an impoverished and lonely way to live. What you do is take the middle road of compromise, accommodation, trade-out. It's the way everyone else is doing it. If you were really to go all out, you'd be seen as an eccentric or oddball. If you take a do-nothing attitude, you are likely to be seen as dull and uninteresting, if not a loser. The safe path is up the middle. You're accepted because you're doing what most everyone else does, neither more nor less.

The 5,5 theory is a "balancing" approach. It's halfway between all of the other possibilities. The theory says in effect, "You have more trouble in the long run if people are driven or disregarded than if you push for the 'what we can get on the average' possibility. You take people's needs into account and over the long term they stay with you."

COMMUNICATION

Under the 5,5 approach to supervision about equal weight is given to formal and informal communication. When formal communication made on behalf of the organization itself is involved, the 5,5 supervisor does make an effort to keep his people posted on what is coming down from the top. From time to time he may shade his interpretation of what the top wants to make it more palatable. But no dishonesty is involved. What he says might not exactly be said the way it was said at the top. Yet if you were the top man and had heard what the 5,5 supervisor was reviewing, you could get the sense of what you had said in the beginning, "I want the project completed by Thursday." Your 5,5 interpreter is saying, "We have an important job here, fellas, and I anticipate some overtime being needed." But then he might go on, "Now, ah, can we commit ourselves to three hours per night?" If they say "No way!" he might negotiate down to 1½ hours and ask them also, "as a personal favor," to come in earlier in the mornings until the crisis is over.

• • •

The department supervisors meeting was about to get underway. John Smoot, the production manager, had called them in to discuss how best to implement policy on administering annual leave. The previous week he had circulated an agenda containing this item, and asking his supervisors to be ready to discuss what the policy-interpretation details should be.

John called the meeting to order and proposed for openers that each supervisor could give a brief account of how he felt the policy should be administered. "How about you leading off, Fred?"

Fred Ware stood up and said, "Well, I tested the policy with my people and about half of them felt we should use seniority as the basis for approving annual leave—and if a tie is encountered here, then we should decide priority on what last year's leave looked like. But the other half feel that 'first come, first served' should be the way to arrange annual leave scheduling, with a seniority basis coming into effect if ties occur."

"Those are two alternatives," the chief remarked, "but are you recommending either of them? Do you have some other proposal for administering annual leave schedules in a way that would keep all departments manned at a proper level? It will also have to be a fair method of deciding between competing 'bids' for vacation slots during the summer when many in the plant would like to be away."

Fred seemed nonplussed for a moment, but then said, "Well, I guess we could combine both suggestions in a way that would be acceptable to everyone, rather than opting for one over the other. Let's see, perhaps seniority for the first round of choices —like someone with 20 years gets first pick before anyone with 19—and then 'first come, first served' for any vacation slots that haven't been filled the other way. How does that sound?"

• • •

This is a 5,5 balancing and trade-off approach, evident from the way this supervisor had begun by testing the policy among his people. Then he had tried to merge both "solutions," making no recommendations as to the weight of one argument over the other, or coming up with ideas of his own. Now he was trying to sell his compromise as a general solution to be applied throughout the plant. In fact, as was pointed out to Fred by the others, the first part of his solution was unworkable, while the second part would hardly connect at all.

As a link in the chain of command, the 5,5 supervisor realizes the importance of passing the word up the ladder. And here again, matters that possibly need to be reported but would produce trouble upstairs are shaped in such a way as to make them more attractive. "There have been some technical problems, sir, and because of various people's home situations, I've had to use judgment in not pressing them on overtime. But several of us are going to try to get going by 7:45. All other things being equal, we hope to finish around Friday noon." Yet, if the

62

top knew how to read it, they would know that the "we won't meet the deadline" message is there embedded in all of the contingencies and tentativeness and provisos, which make it so difficult to get at.

The informal level of communication does not *belong* to the organization, but in many ways it's *about* it, involving grapevine, scuttlebutt, rumors, hearsay, as well as a good deal of out-of-field talking that's not pertinent to the organization's purposes. These include everything from sports events of the weekend to the most recent political development.

The 5,5 supervisor's interest in informal communication is that it's an open window into the pulse of the people, how they are feeling, what's disturbing them, pressure points that worry them, and so on. By keeping his antenna out and knowing all these things, the 5,5 supervisor is in a position to take many different kinds of actions. He can float a contradictory rumor in order to block one he's heard and doesn't like, or he can use what he knows is being passed in the informal communication network as the basis for timing either good or bad messages from on high. Beyond that, of course, by the 5,5 supervisor "keeping in touch," he frequently is able to pass information up that permits higher levels of management to initiate corrective actions concerning matters that would have a bad effect on organization productivity if left unattended.

It terms of what has been said, the 5,5 kind of supervisor is in a go-between position. He runs between the formal and the informal systems and keeps himself oriented to what's been done in the past, trying to figure out what the consequences of a course of action would be, first from one side and then from the other. By a series of corrections he finally can find a position which will get the job done in a "reasonably" good manner without stirring up too much trouble. But often it seems less trouble to rely on the "tried and true" answers given by traditions, precedents and past practices.

• • •

The female work force in an established insurance company

used to be almost one hundred percent clerical and non-technical/professional. Salary grades in this area are minimal and there is high personnel turnover. It is common for a female basic-grade clerical employee not to return to work after taking maternity leave. However, in recent years, the non-clerical specialist and managerial female proportion of the work force has been increasing.

Betty Blain, the company's only woman actuary, became pregnant. She had been with the company more than three years and had recently completed her professional qualification. But as woman rather than actuary, company policy stipulated she had to be released from duty not less than four weeks prior to the expected date of her delivery. Normally she would not return to work less than six weeks after delivery, unless her doctor gave her specific permission to do so. Because so many of the mothers never returned, the company had abolished paid maternity leave long ago. It would pay only sick leave and annual leave. An employee on maternity leave would have to use her cumulative unused sick leave first. If she had insufficient sick leave days to cover the ten weeks or more away, she would then be charged annual leave. If that still didn't cover the absence, she would be granted leave without pay.

Betty did not have sufficient sick and annual leave to preclude use of leave without pay; but as she put it, "Chandler and I sure could use the money while I'm going through this." The supervisory problem thus became one of how to handle the situation to the employee's best advantage as well as that of the company of which she was a valued contributing member. The chief actuary pored through the policy manual and found that it provided for advancing sick leave when needed. So he decided that when Betty's sick and annual leave had expired, the absence record would reflect use of advanced sick leave to cover the remaining time away.

When the attendance report was received in the payroll office, Myra, the payroll supervisor, made a call to the chief. She flatly stated that sick leave could not be advanced in maternity cases. The chief actuary asked why. His interpretation of the policy manual indicated that while historically it had not often been done, there was nothing to indicate that it *could not* be done. Myra came back with, "Well, it can't be done because it has just never been done before."

• • •

This was a 5,5 communication because of the payroll supervisor's reliance on tradition, precedents, and past practices as indicating a "solution," rather than considering Betty's own situation as the problem to be resolved to the extent permissible under company policy.

GIVING DIRECTIONS

As might be concluded from what has been said about communication, the 5,5 supervisor uses communications to get his work done. To avoid being pushy, he requests and tries to persuade and sell. It's a fairly soft sell, without being too mushy. Furthermore, he gives directions in a tentative manner to see what kind of reactions people will have. If they buy it, well and good; if they have objections, his manner of being tentative about what he has said makes it possible to back off and test another course of action. As a result, a 5,5 supervisor directs the work of his subordinates more in general terms than down to specific details. He does this by explaining aims and schedules, ensuring that subordinates are agreeable to what is being proposed. Also, he makes more things more acceptable by ensuring that each subordinate feels free to come back if he needs any help in carrying out the work.

You might say, then, that the 5,5 supervisor keeps his finger on the tempo that people are ready to adopt. He doesn't try to speed it up but rather accepts the situation as is. Then he offers direction in a general and tentative way, using persuasion to gain acceptance, but maintaining tentativeness so that he can always back off if what he suggests is rejected.

• • •

Jim James, Capital County's supervisor of highway mainten-

ance, was sitting around a table with most of the members of
his crew, waiting for two o'clock to arrive so they could start
their special meeting. Jim's chief, Con Bales, had informed him
earlier that because the newly elected Mayor and his wife were
very beautification conscious, he had to start preparing his
crew members to undertake tree and flower planting along with
their other duties in the county. This would also entail mowing
grass and creating lawn areas at scenic points favored by the
Mayor's attentions.

Jim was a little worried. He had a fairly good idea regarding
how his highway employees would react to this proposition.
Mrs. Moffitt's beautification plans had already been widely pub-
licized, and recently he had heard several remarks that the additional work load would be too great.

Jim called the meeting to order at two o'clock and opened
by asking, "What would you say if we talked about starting to
do a little landscaping now and then as we work through our
usual program? I know several of you are keen gardeners—now
you can indulge your hobby on county time and get paid for
it." Immediately there were complaints from several of the
men, mainly that it wasn't part of their job and they were overloaded anyway.

Jim responded, "Well, we're going to have to do something
about it, she's cruising around our county all the time. The
Mayor's really been pushing the Commission, and I've been requested to get ready for round-the-year highway beautification.
Would you fellas buy it on a 'work load permitting' basis?"

• • •

This is a 5,5 approach to giving directions because the supervisor was acting more or less in a tentative "balancing" response
to rumors and feedback he was receiving. He believed in "testing the wind" before stating a specific position. When he encountered resistance, he edged toward a compromise position
that would at least partially satisfy his subordinates as well as
his own boss and the Mayor.

In many ways, 5,5 balancing between production-people

considerations has to involve splitting somewhere between all the way and nothing much at all in order to come out with something that's "practically achievable," as the supervisor puts it. There is one particular angle on splitting which deserves far more attention than it's had. It comes up whenever a person's own ethics or moral standards tell him that something should be done one way, but "the system" or his boss tells him to do it another.

The 5,5 way out of such a dilemma is to "split" this difference between two moral codes by telling oneself, "I'm not being paid to do what's right, sound, ethical and proper by *my* standards. That being so, I'm justified in parking my personal beliefs outside during working hours, just as I do with my car. Then I can apply myself in good conscience to do what the organization thinks should be done. Of course, I may feel a few twinges at times. But basically, as long as I'm what *they* want, I'm covered."

Such is the 5,5 approach to resolving ethical dilemmas. Once it gets started in an organization it's hard to stop, and the long-term damage to sound behavior can be great, however many 5,5 people are saying, "To make it in this outfit, you have to stay 'on the team' and do it their way."

MANAGING MISTAKES AND ERRORS

A 5,5 supervisor knows, human nature being what it is, that mistakes and errors are inevitable. They can never be eliminated and if you put people under pressure to do so, you may only cause more mistakes to be made. The goal then in managing mistakes and errors is to create a relaxed environment rather than a tense one. This can be done not by winking or hiding his head in the sand like an ostrich, but by always coming up on the employee's side and giving him the benefit of the doubt, the first few times at least. He knows no subordinate ever intended to make a mistake. He appreciates that people are embarrassed when they have to admit having made one.

Since mistakes and errors can often be traced to insufficient or inadequate training, a 5,5 supervisor encourages special courses that can help his people do a better job. He also knows that mistakes and errors often happen because people take shortcuts, but he encourages them to stick with traditions, precedents, and past practices, operating regulations, manuals, and so on, at least to the degree that other people do. This may slow productivity down but it is a good way to get mistakes and errors under better control. Furthermore, a 5,5 supervisor is as embarrassed as anyone else if he has to admit that mistakes were made because he failed to employ rules and procedures. So as a result he is likely to stay close to them and ask his people to do so. Then if a mistake does occur, at least he won't be blamed for exercising too little control over performance deviations.

Organizations managed in a 5,5 way are likely to be quite bureaucratic. The reason is that people have learned the importance of adhering to rules, regulations, and red tape.

The 5,5 supervisory approach, then, for managing mistakes and errors is first of all to keep the tempo at an easy pace so that people are not under pressure. Then if mistakes occur and if he can—but not forever—he gives the subordinate the benefit of the doubt. Finally, the 5,5 supervisor encourages his subordinates to work according to rules, traditions, precedents, past practices and to standard operating procedures, and so on. This is not necessarily done literally, but in the sense of staying close enough so that shortcuts that might produce mistakes and errors can be avoided. Then if something does go wrong, he at least has the possibility of avoiding criticism from his own boss for sloppy supervision.

• • •

Bob Drake, a section head in Contract Estimates, hung up his phone with his ear still burning due to a lecture he had just received from his boss about inappropriate routing of important customer correspondence. On three occasions during the last month correspondence had been misrouted. Each foul-up caused an embarrassing and perhaps near-disastrous situation because needed coordination within the office concerning contract bids and their deadlines was missed.

Bob shoved back his chair and went to his outer office to take up the matter with his secretary, Mae Grimshaw, who he thought was responsible for the problems. Over the last month he had noticed that she hadn't looked too well and that she had been making more and more mistakes. He had overheard her making snappish remarks on the phone as well.

Clearing his throat to get her attention, he began, "Mae, you are going to have to watch this correspondence routing a little closer. I just got chewed out by the division chief about three different routing errors that have occurred in the last month. I would really appreciate it if you'd try to be a little more careful. I know you're doing a good job and trying real hard. I'm also aware you haven't been your normal self the past month, but I sure would appreciate your giving more effort to this area." Mae looked at him rather weakly, shrugged her shoulders, and said she would do the best she could. Bob turned around and walked back into the inner office. Soon he heard the sound of quiet sobbing. "It's a sad situation all around," he reflected, "but I had to check her before things got much worse." He turned to some paperwork which would not involve calling her in for some time.

• • •

This was a 5,5 response to managing mistakes in that the boss gave only surface treatment to what evidently is a work problem being aggravated by a more deepseated human problem. He didn't make an effort to dig into what the associated misrouting and personal problems were. Instead, he "spoke to her about it" as a mild reprimand. In that way he covered his tracks and had something to report back to his boss if challenged later about whether or not he had followed up on the mistakes.

DEALING WITH COMPLAINTS

A 5,5 supervisor responds to complaints. He realizes that failure to deal with them can have a bad effect on the steady, continuing productivity he wants. The 5,5 boss really believes in the "open-door" policy. Anybody who works for him has access to him in private at any time on any topic. He hopes in this way subordinates will be encouraged to get off their chests anything that's worrying them. When they come to him, he will be in the best position to deal with whatever tensions have arisen and to prevent them building up to a crisis.

But he finds some complaints difficult to answer because they refer to matters over which he has no control. When this kind of complaint is lodged he is likely to talk it over with the subordinate and help him to see it in a different light. Looked at from this other way, the problem does not seem so important as it had appeared at first. When he can't do that, he is likely to move in a tentative direction and say, "Let me take it up with my boss and see if anything can be done about it." Then when he comes back, if he had any success at all, he can offer perhaps a compromise solution giving the subordinate some concession which answers his complaint in part. "Half a loaf is better than none" is a proverb frequently quoted by the 5,5 boss. Another of his strategies for dealing with complaints is to trade out. The boss might say, "Look, I'm really sorry. That's something I can't do anything about. However, there is something I *can* do that I believe would be helpful to you, and I would like to do it as a personal way of making amends for the difficulty you're in."

So the 5,5 boss really is sensitive to complaints. They're disturbing to him because they signal troubles people are having which could impede production. On the other hand, they could result in his being criticized by his own boss for being ineffective in solving problems of subordinates that affect their morale.

By being available to people and by responding to a complaint if possible, or managing to blunt its sharpness by compromise strategies, a 5,5 supervisor is often—but not always—able to create a "live and let live" kind of climate.

• • •

Jim Smith, the field supervisor at Centerville, was sitting at his desk when Peter Rollinson, one of his oilfield technicians, came in and angrily threw down on Jim's desk the slip from Personnel which indicated he had been ranked "highly qualified" on a selection list for the supervisor vacancy at Crab Key. His bid, however, had not been referred as one of the three names that went to the final selection panel. Jim had yet to read the slip. "Sit down, Peter—I guess you have something on your mind." Peter did sit down, but he already felt Jim had put him down with that flippant remark. Nonetheless, he was in Jim's office to get justice—against whatever odds.

Peter went through a long story. He had done all those things Jim had told him to do that would make him competitive for a supervisory position. He had voluntarily taken a number of supervisory training courses, as well as all the refresher technical training that was required or otherwise had come his way. In addition, he had added to his certification credentials at a number of other facilities, and considered himself highly qualified for the position for which he had bid.

"You're a good, competent technician, Peter, one of the best I have," Jim said in reply. "I'd like to keep you with me. . . ." "Is *that* why you didn't support me?" Peter interrupted furiously.

"Hear me out, Pete. Let's look at some realities. Crab Key is one of the most popular locations in the region, so that job you were after would have been highly competitive. Let's face it— there were people who bid on that position who probably wouldn't bid on any other. This is one of the reasons you might not have made the list. There would be others too."

"*What* others?"

"Well, the Crab Key opportunity is gone now, but perhaps you should consider taking some night work in college, Peter." Jim went on to mention that merit awards probably were a big factor and that Peter had not earned any in the past few years. Perhaps he should consider trying to work a little harder and maybe get some recognition in that manner.

While Jim had been talking, he had watched Peter's face and general demeanor to see how each argument was "playing." But this was one of those days—no luck whatever. Jim ran a few more persuasive suggestions, but within a few minutes the technician stood up and said flatly, "You can't sell me, Jim. I've worked my tail off for you, the results are documented. I deserve better than you can bring yourself to recommend me for —I've wondered why, but now, who cares? So I'm taking the whole deal upstairs through channels!"

• • •

This is a 5,5-supervised situation because Jim has merely been attempting to pacify Peter by suggesting he accept the status quo and look at some ways he might consider for improvement and not getting down to the facts to determine what the real problem might be. Jim's actual but never revealed motives for wanting to keep Peter are open to question.

REACTING TO HOSTILE FEELINGS

Hostile feelings worry a 5,5 supervisor. They make him anxious. He doesn't think well on his feet under the emotional pressure that's involved. A reason for this is that to balance production and people concerns, the supervisor feels he needs stable conditions. When hostility erupts, it's as though the ground beneath his balancing scales is trembling and putting them out of kilter.

Given these circumstances, how does a 5,5 supervisor react when first confronted by a person expressing hostile feelings? He will do one or more of several things. First, he'll try to keep the conversation fairly superficial so as to avoid a situation where the person expressing hostile feelings would become extremely upset. He attempts to focus the conversation on operational matters which are always easier to discuss. Second, the 5,5 supervisor does his very best to avoid expressing hostile feelings toward the subordinate if this can possibly be done. The reason is that if he were to do so, the situation could degenerate into win-lose, and that kind of a battle is definitely something that a 5,5 supervisor wishes to avoid. Third, if a subordinate has come to him in a rage, the supervisor might make a move to get a cooling-off period during which he can think over what to do. He might do this by saying, "I very much appreciate your telling me these things. They're important to me. Rather than giving you a quick reaction, I'd like an opportunity to ponder these matters and turn them over in my mind. I wonder if we could get together next Monday." By using this strategy the supervisor not only gains time to think, but also the chances are good that the subordinate will cool off during the interim. Thus, when they get back together the fury may have died away, or if it hasn't, at least the boss is in a position to offer the subordinate alternative ways of thinking about possibly solving the problem that has aroused his hostile feelings. This is a splitting technique. It has in it much the same basic thinking as in other 5,5 supervisory techniques that involve compromise, adjustment, and accommodation.

• • •

Bernice James, a saleslady at Lilly's Shoppe, burst through the door from the fitting room with a silk blouse clutched in both hands, shook it several times, then ripped it from end to end. Her supervisor, Anne Johnson, turned, startled at the outburst. She walked over and picked up the torn remnants. "What seems to be bugging you?" she inquired. Bernice began spluttering, "that crude sarcastic . . . ."

"So she gave you a bad time," Anne summarized. She went on, "Bernice, you really ought to find a better way to blow off steam after having a difficult customer—maybe hit your head against the door or something. Look what you've done to this valuable blouse—it's a write-off. You know you could be fired for deliberately destroying merchandise?"

"I guess so. It was stupid of me, but at the time. . . . Anne, you should have heard that character needling me and putting me down. I stayed polite even after she'd asked me if I was Mary Poppins. But I was boiling inside, and as soon as she'd gone, it had to blow somehow."

"Let's go back to the floor, Bernice." As they left the stock room, Anne reached into a bin, took out another silk blouse and handed it over, saying, "Why don't you see if you can stop yourself from tearing up expensive items and we'll let it go this time. Only don't let it happen again."

• • •

This is 5,5 because the supervisor is taking a "balancing" approach in regard to hostile feelings. She is not particularly interested in getting to the basis of the saleswoman's feelings and on the other hand less than fully interested in taking action in response to an obvious violation of good practices regarding merchandise. After Bernice's destructive outburst, Anne begins by putting weight on the "disciplinary sanctions" aspect. A little later, she balances this off by giving Bernice a "break"—that is, by emphasizing that although she *could* institute termination, this time she won't—on condition that Bernice tries not to mishandle merchandise in the future. It is a managed "trade off" outcome. Anne has not found the kind of solution possible from investigation of a problem's causes.

The 5,5 supervisory approach to reacting to hostile feelings, then, is to acknowledge their existence and treat them as having importance. The goal is to try to relieve the hostile tensions in administrative ways. This can be done by suggesting alternative possibilities or by diverting the hostile feelings as the conversation is guided into operational issues that can be discussed with greater objectivity. They can be postponed to be rid of them by suggesting that a fuller discussion take place in a few days' time so that "both of us" (especially the supervisor) can think things over before returning to it.

The subordinate is unlikely to feel he is on a full and open exchange-of-views basis with his boss when the supervisor deals with his hostile feelings in this manner. Nonetheless, the subordinate is aware he has been listened to and his hostile feelings have been taken into account and are being given pertinent consideration.

PERFORMANCE REVIEW AND EVALUATION

When the 5,5 supervisor is setting goals with his subordinate for the period ahead, the motto is "Let's be realistic." After all, he reasons, these targets are going to be a matter of record, documented in a way that permits his *own* boss to bring them up as part of a review of supervisory performance. So basically, as seen from this angle, the 5,5 supervisor and his subordinate have a common interest in not "overreaching" themselves. The supervisor guides the discussion so as to accommodate both his and the subordinate's views of what is possible. Usually they commit themselves to a quite moderate written-down estimate. At the time these goals are set, they feel they wouldn't be surprised if, by the end of the period, the goals were exceeded. That would be praiseworthy, but in any event, they have a bull's-eye that's "certain" to be hit.

By the end of the period, as so often happens, results may be below target. In the followup interview, both the boss and his subordinate, looking back, conclude they must have been overoptimistic, not having forecast and taken into account that numerous difficulties and delays actually occurred. Even though boss and subordinate are now formally accountable to higherups for the gap between promise and performance, the 5,5 supervisor is somewhat of an expert in subtly "shifting the bull's-eye" so that after the event it seems to be exactly where the spent arrow of effort has landed.

• • •

Jane Dowling, a supply clerk, had continually been making recording errors and failing to keep the records up to date. Her inventory management was also unsatisfactory. Jane's position description requires that records be maintained accurately and on time and that inventory control be up to date.

Sam Hays, Jane's supervisor, had mentioned the deficiencies with Jane on several previous occasions during the year and made suggestions as to what should be done to bring her performance up to an acceptable level. Sam and Jane had agreed that the next Monday at 2:00 in his office they would have the annual performance review. Jane arrived at Sam's office promptly. The interview commenced.

Sam began by telling Jane, "Your performance as a whole is in the satisfactory area but you still need some improvement. Maybe you should pay more attention to making record entries. Let's work on improving this area. Is that okay with you?"

Jane replied, "I've been doing my best but I don't think I can improve much more. No one can be one hundred percent accurate."

Sam responded, "Well, let's try to make *some* progress even though it might not be possible to get up to standards quickly."

• • •

This is a 5,5 "let's see if it plays"/"half a loaf" approach. The supervisor was indirect both in getting to the first performance evaluation topic to be discussed and in pointing out the specific improvements needed. Also, as the performance evaluation began, the supervisor started the typical 5,5 alternation between "In this way you're quite good—but in another area you might consider improving." The 5,5 assumption is that by creating an ongoing "sandwich" of "a little of the good, then a little of the bad," a supervisor's "small steps of improvement" personnel evaluation and review emphasis will be made more palatable for the subordinate. The 5,5 approach to performance review and evaluation can well be called the "sandwich" technique.

What this means is that the boss prepares in advance for the performance review or annual interview, and then, having clear in mind what he wants to say—particularly those aspects which are of a negative character—he proceeds in the following manner. The initial evaluation begins with a "positive" aspect of the subordinate's performance.. Then the supervisor brings up a negative point said in the "best" way he can. Even if tensions are aroused, he quickly moves to another area where he hopefully can "balance in" another complimentary evaluation. So in this approach each negative remark is tucked in between two positive ones, and the thought is that by doing so, whatever sting it might have contained will be taken out.

A second approach to performance review and evaluation discussions by a 5,5 supervisor is to invite the subordinate at the beginning of the interview to offer self-evaluations. When he does so, and particularly if he comments upon negative aspects of his own behavior, in this manner the boss nods or otherwise gives his quiet acknowledgment of the critical remark. The subordinate is not offended because it is he who said it. The boss' reaction that he receives is less harsh than he may have feared. He may even feel good about the boss who, rather than "criticizing him," is letting him go about improving under his own steam. But when the subordinate thinks it all over later, he could feel that since very little of a negative sort was emphasized, he need attach little or no weight to the self-criticism, whether or not the boss agreed with it.

A third 5,5 approach to performance evaluation is this. The 5,5 supervisor can walk the subordinate back along the memory trail to a situation that contained the negative aspect of behavior that the boss wants to be recognized. Then, many times, the boss will find the subordinate acknowledging that "sure enough, that's a problem I didn't handle too well." The person has not been asked outright to make a self-appraisal, but for all practical purposes, he has been led into a situation where self-appraisal is inevitable. Again, the criticism is accomplished without the supervisor being put in the role of a critic.

The underlying theme of 5,5 performance evaluation is that the supervisor tries in indirect ways to bring the subordinate's attention to matters of relevance for his improvement. The "indirect" aspect is meant to prevent the relationships between boss and subordinate from becoming polarized in a way that would produce antagonisms and win-lose disagreements. Any performance deficiencies not identified in this manner are likely to be tabled by the boss. He doesn't try to get them into the conversation, sometimes on the rationalization to himself that, "We covered a lot and dug deeply into several significant issues. But a person can only tolerate a certain amount of criticism, and going beyond that limit isn't a sound thing to do. Had I asked him to consider that other aspect of his behavior, it would have been too much. Next year perhaps."

SUMMARY

A 5,5 supervisory approach is where the boss adjusts himself to the system and to the comfortable tempo that others have come to adopt. He doesn't push for more even though results obtained are less than what might have been accomplished by a different approach to supervision. In this way progress is made and the boss can feel that at least he did turn in a half loaf. The supervisor relies on tradition, precedent, and past practice, standard operating procedures, regulations, and so on, but with these interpreted "sensibly," rather than implemented in a literal way. In this manner, the work is done according to the spirit if not the letter of the law. When differences do arise between the boss and his subordinates they are relieved to the extent possible by splitting the difference in ways that include compromise, accommodation, and adjustment. In terms of specific elements of management, the 5,5 approach can be summarized as follows.

1. A 5,5 supervisor is interested in and attentive to problems of management that can be solved by thoughtful communication. He realizes that he is a go-between, responsible for passing information up about subordinate morale, attitudes, feelings, concerns, and so on, as well as passing management concerns down. The 5,5 supervisor uses the formal communication channels in terms of regular meetings, memoranda, bulletin boards, etc., but in addition pays close attention to informal communication, examples of which are rumors, scuttlebutt, and gripes. His goal is to anticipate difficulties and in this way to avoid them through effective communication.

2. Directions are given in a general manner rather than in specific terms, and in this way, subordinates are unlikely to feel excessive pressure. The boss makes himself available to give help whenever subordinates feel they need it and request it. In this easy give-and-take way performance is

accomplished, not necessarily at a high level but to an acceptable degree.

3. Mistakes and errors are seen as inevitable. But if they are not handled in a "sound" manner, acrimony and antagonism can result. One way of avoiding them is to encourage subordinates to work according to long-established practices or as set down in operating manuals, not to the literal letter, but within appropriate guidelines. In this way errors from shortcuts are avoided, although gains from discovering new innovative practices are sacrificed. At first, and for a limited number of repeats of the same mistake, the 5,5 boss gives subordinates the benefit of the doubt.

4. Reacting to complaints is a very delicate matter and the 5,5 boss seeks ways of keeping emotions from erupting. He may attempt to do this by channeling a discussion into administrative areas or by introducing cooling-off periods that give him a time to think and that also allow the hostile feelings to fade out.

5. Performance review and evaluation are carried out in such a manner as to, hopefully, get the subordinate himself to acknowledge his faults and promise to rectify them. In this way the boss avoids being openly critical, because the subordinate is unlikely to feel that the boss is holding him responsible about those matters which he himself has admitted to be unsatisfactory in his performance up to now. Otherwise, sandwich techniques of embedding criticism between compliments are employed to take the sting away.

The 5,5 approach to supervision is a safe and widely used set of assumptions and related techniques. It is safe because it does get people to "perform," not to a high degree but to an acceptable amount, and it does avoid people problems—though again, not entirely. It is a fairly successful way of keeping production and people requirements on an even keel if, as belief has it, "too much" of one means "too little" of the other.

CHAPTER 6

9,9

The 9,9 Grid style is located in the upper right corner of
Figure 1. This is where a 9 of concern for results meets a 9 of
concern for people. It's the theory that says, "Through getting
their active participation, you can earn the involvement and
commitment of people to find and use the best solutions in
everyday work. Only through participation, involvement, and
commitment is it really possible to achieve high results. Those
who are supervised in a 9,9 way want to win and the measure
of winning is that results are truly excellent."

The 9,9 way of managing takes more skill in personal leadership and teamwork development than do other styles. The supervisor is a leader in two ways. From one angle he helps subordinates to see possibilities they might not see as being open to
them without his leadership. His way of leading is to help people to set high goals which are attainable only through committed effort. The other leadership feature is to use to the fullest
the resources that subordinates can contribute in achieving
such goals.

Various lines of evidence lead to the conclusion that 9,9 is
beginning to replace 9,1 and other supervisory strategies. When
authority-obedience environments began to crumble, supervisors started leaving the 9,1 corner. Some took the soft solution
of 1,9. Others went the route of compromise, accommodation
and adjustment characteristic of 5,5. Still others, in these confused circumstances, threw their hands up in a 1,1 way, seeing

the whole deal as hopeless but still wanting to hang in there until they could get retirement benefits.

As the Grid has made clear, there is a common belief shared by the 9,1; 1,9 and 5,5 approaches even though in other respects they are as different as iron, honey, and skim milk. The shared belief is that more results can or could be attained only at the expense of people. Each of the three styles looks at this supposed issue through its own lenses. 9,1 takes a hard-eyed squint and says, "We've *gotta* have more results. If I considered people's feelings there'd be less. So feelings don't count around here." 1,9 peers through rose-colored prisms and concludes, "Brutal demands for results are both wrong and self-defeating. A supervisor who really cares has to promote positive feelings from the beginning. Then I can have hopes that production will follow as the harvest of sincere and kind personal cultivation of my people." A 5,5 supervisor looks through his bifocals and says, "It's dangerous to go too far either way when you're trying to accomplish production through people. Not too little, not too much, but 'just right' balanced emphasis on both scales is the practical way to supervise." The problem is "hidden" from a 1,1 supervisor, because his glasses don't permit him to see.

All of these propositions take for granted an "either/or," or a "neither" attitude. They set up a *false* issue and abide by its indications. Drop the assumption that high concern for production inevitably cancels out high concern for people, and what do you get? The two high concerns not only can coexist but also can be unified! This is where 9,9 takes off.

There is one other point that needs to be made early about 9,9 teamwork. Teamwork does not mean all members working physically together within sight-and-sound range of one another all the time. Far from it. Let's say a team has four members. Tom is boss; subordinates are Dick, Harry and Bill. Some "team" problems involve only Tom—or only Dick or Harry or Bill—in their solutions. Then it's in the interest of teamwork for the individual member to solve the problem himself, and his effectiveness in doing so contributes to teamwork by avoid-

FIGURE 2

Guidelines for Three Approaches to 9,9 Team Action

Conditions	One-Alone	One-to-One	One-to-All
Time	unavailable	available	available
Judgmental competence	full	insufficient	insufficient
Pooling of information	none needed	vertically only	needed both horizontally and vertically
Whose problem is it?	mine	his; both of us	ours
Can others add anything?	no	yes	yes
Involvement-commitment	no significance	helpful-essential	necessary-essential
Implications for others	none	present	present
Understanding by others of purpose	no problem or can be assumed	needed	needed
Coordination of effort	unnecessary	vertical only	horizontal and vertical
Followup	unnecessary	necessary	necessary
Management development potential	none	present	present
Synergy	irrelevant	possible	possible

ing duplication of effort. Some "team" problems, in other words, are "one-alone" (1/0).

Other "team" problems involve Tom and Dick together, since Harry and others can contribute nothing to the solution. It's up to Tom and Dick to work out the solution between themselves. These "one-to-one" (1/1) circumstances make it possible to free others who can contribute nothing to use their time and effort dealing with other aspects of the team situation.

Some, however, can only be solved by Tom, Dick, Harry,

and Bill working as a unit. Such team situations are "one-to-all" (1/all).

Those who have tried the 9,9 way of supervision have found it to be the key management style for today, tomorrow, and the years ahead whether the problem is a 1/0, 1/1 or 1/all situation. Now, what are the more specific characteristics of what 9,9 is in practice?

Figure 2 indicates the particular conditions under which 1/0, or 1/1, or 1/all constitute 9,9 team management. The left-hand column specifies a number of conditions that aid a manager to evaluate when 1/0, 1/1, or 1/all are likely to be 9,9 actions.

COMMUNICATION

A 9,9 supervisor communicates to promote understanding and to earn the agreement of his subordinates for actions to be taken. Authentic communication is basic to achieving these communication goals. What does this mean? For starters it means that he doesn't alter the message that needs to be understood just to make it easy to swallow. He is factual and applies no sugar-coating. Then, he doesn't just put out the word in a way that leaves people to pick it up or not as they wish. Neither does he shove the message down people's throats as an edict. Nor does he use a public relations approach by trying to make things look more positive than they are or charming his subordinates by his own powers of persuasion.

What he does is to present problems in the most honest, realistic, and objective terms he is capable of. This means he describes any given problem in terms of what the current difficulty being encountered is, what he sees to be the cause of it, and what he sees to be the oncoming consequences. He may also indicate possible solutions if he has clear-cut ideas as to what a good solution might be.

• • •

A tornado had just touched down and passed through the outskirts of Plainway. From the moment it swept through the power transmission switching station outside of town, electric power became nonexistent. At Plainway Savings and Loan, it was like being transported back a hundred years as all lights went off, the computer went down, and every adding machine went dead. The S&L, which was partway through a long conversion program from mechanized accounting to full EDP operation, did not yet possess a standby generator. The only device still working was a battery powered radio which had been giving out emergency weather bulletins and other public service information. As Frank O'Brien, Plainway's installment loan supervisor, began taking stock of the situation, a news flash came through to the effect that power had been knocked out entirely and it might take a day or more to get the switching station and its feeder transmission lines repaired and operating.

The weather was clearing, some customers were already at the windows and Frank had no reason to doubt that others would be along soon, since little or no property damage had been reported within the city limits. A decision came down from his boss by messenger: "We'll stay open. Do your best." He had already checked with the tellers, who were continuing as usual to give written receipts only in respect to payments that were not made by check. Their adding-listing machines for making periodic totals of checks and cash for balancing against receipts were out of service, but that was a minor problem— ". . . could have been much worse if we'd gotten to on-line account posting by now," Frank reflected. He instructed the tellers to continue for the time being with all windows open rather than following their usual timetable of one window at a time closing temporarily to balance and collate a batch of transactions to be keypunched onto cards as input data for computer posting. The big trouble today would be with postings. He picked up the phone, found it dead, and then hurried to the computer section where the small group of operators stood, unshaken by the technology shut-down.

"What the heck do we do now, beyond buying more candles?" Joe Sullivan asked.

"Well, we're staying open for business and the tellers have

resumed, so we can expect checks and receipt copies to be coming through as usual for posting. If power is out for a day or two, as seems likely, there could be one whale of a backlog unless we do some hand posting and analysis."

"But how do we do that?" Millie, the junior keypunch operator, inquired in genuine amazement. "I can change a tire but I can't shoe a horse."

"Don't worry, we have an edge over *that* situation," Frank assured her, "since the same accounting principles apply in EDP and hand methods."

"Yes, but with four of us, how do we keep up?" Helen asked. "Why, I used to come in here with Mom when she was paying off the mortgage back in the old days. There used to be lines of desks and a small army of bookkeepers posting to account cards."

"Hey, there's *got* to be some of those cards down in the archives!" Joe exclaimed. "Even some unused ones maybe. Old Herb Smallwood, who retired a couple of years ago, would have stashed them away—let's bring him in. He'll be glad to help out, it'll be like old times for him."

"Yes, and he's president of the Retirees Club, isn't he? He'll know some others from the old bookkeeping days who might come in. . . ."

A solution took shape. Frank got temporary-help authorization from his boss and dispatched Millie with a note to Herb asking for his and other Club members' help. By noon, tables and chairs had been set up in a roped-off section of the foyer; Herb had arrived and had broken out some stored boxes of unused account cards from the golden age of bookkeeping. Between welcoming and installing members of his old posting section, he helped Frank set up the temporary classifications and control accounts needed for by-hand analysis. Meanwhile, Helen had gone to an office equipment firm and rented its few remaining hand-cranked adding-listing machines.

In a cheerful and dedicated "Let's beat out the computer" mood, the old-timers worked with remarkable speed and accuracy through the afternoon and evening to post and balance by candlelight the day's installment loan transactions. Joe, Helen, and Millie helped Frank pick up from yesterday's closing balances printout and reconcile the control accounts so as to reach an overall closing balance of today's business. Frank also saw to it that the retirees dined at Plainway's expense in a nearby restaurant, and he had a reporter and photographer come by to record for publication in the local newspaper, after power was restored the next day, how the Retirees Club had come to the rescue.

• • •

This is a 9,9 approach because the supervisor picked up the ball and related the major problem—how to keep up with account postings and analysis—to his computer operators and got them involved in its solution. Another feature of the 9,9 approach can be seen in the way that the supervisor arranged for the city's newspaper to make known to Plainway's community the splendid contribution by Plainway retirees in helping the S&L through its power blackout difficulties. That's communication.

As the boss presents and discusses his views, subordinates don't feel they are being sold a bill of goods. Rather from what he says they can come to understand what the problem is as he sees it. Then if they see it in a different way than he does, subordinates are in an excellent position to get the boss to see whatever limitations there might be in his own understanding of the problem. They can do this by pointing out what the differences are between how he describes the problem and how they understand it. For example, they might point out unjustified assumptions he may be making. To convince him, they can do this by identifying facts that "could not be so" under the terms of one or more faulty assumptions. To illustrate, perhaps the boss presently believes that a certain work activity should be discontinued because it's not helping productivity. Then someone points out and explains the useful purpose he sees it serving. If this is clearly proved to be the case, the boss will change his mind.

If the boss' opening definition of the problem squares with what they understand the situation to be, then agreement on action can quickly be reached. In this kind of give-and-take, respect comes from authoritative knowledge of the problem, grasp of facts and data, ability to see connections between things, and awareness of which approach toward the solution would have the best consequences. That's really authority. It's not authority based on rank. It is authority based on knowledge and used in contributions. The 9,9 supervisor who leads has no need to dominate the discussion or to use his rank. His need is to get agreement on what the best solution is among those who must implement it. 9,9 skill is in helping others express themselves and think through options and alternatives so that the best answer emerges above the others. Whether the best answer comes from the boss or a subordinate is not important. What is important is that the best answer is identified and used.

This means a premium is placed on the boss' skill in listening and his openness and receptivity to ideas presented by others. His goal is to get each of these ideas well defined and understood so that it can be evaluated in the light of logically connected facts and forecasts. Then if the idea is right, it can be used. But if it isn't, the person who presented it can see, in terms of actual evidence, what the shortcomings of his idea are. Then he can abandon it without loss of face. The 9,9 boss listens to subordinates to understand the ideas they are attempting to sketch in words. He doesn't listen in order to agree; he listens in order to gain understanding before he or anyone else comments. Their contribution and his are put together and tested as the best approach is being sought.

Under these circumstances, subordinates realize that discussions have an open quality. By the boss himself being open and receptive, his subordinates can readily learn the values of being open and receptive. By the boss being authentic, holding back nothing that is significant, subordinates come to know too that candor on their part is welcome and put to constructive use. Among members of a 9,9 work team, communication has an authentic quality. It is most recognizable by contrast with the "double meaning" conversations between members of a group who are not being frank with one another. Team members feel free to be open with one another as they solve problems together. Their discussions are lively. In comparison, a discussion group of closed and mutually distrustful individuals echoes the hollowness hidden beneath the surface aspects of its functioning.

9,9-oriented communication promotes an "everybody wins" kind of situation because it creates the strongest likelihood that each person's knowledge and skills will be brought into participation. This means, too, that team members feel directly involved in the problem's solution. By the very fact of their participation, the solution becomes *genuine* and thus earns their full commitment to implementing it.

GIVING DIRECTIONS

Under 9,9 supervision, giving directions is also quite different from any other approach. Basic to this difference is that goals and objectives will already have been created, shared, and understood through the team's problem-solving and communication process that is built and maintained with 9,9 leadership.

When each subordinate knows the team goals, as well as the specific goals he himself is responsible for accomplishing, then giving directions takes on a unique character. The idea really is to make it unnecessary to give frequent directions of the "Now do *this*, next do that. . . " "masterminding" variety. By getting team agreement and understanding on what goals and objectives are important to accomplish and developing next-step agreements on best strategies and tactics for the team to accomplish those objectives in full coordination or one-to-one or through one-alone actions, "direction" becomes self-evident.

Key to this difference in giving directions is replacement of authority-obedience concepts by involvement-participation-commitment concepts. When subordinates have participated in thinking through with their supervisor as to what objectives and goals are important to accomplish, there is already involvement in the problem. Participants become committed to the strategy and tactics of action through which such goals and objectives are to be pursued. They know what to do, as a team or each in his own right.

Thus, the boss' role is that of keeping the "from here to there" gap between present realities of progress and the to-be-attained goal accomplishment in focus as the gap is being narrowed and closed. His job is to maintain involvement rather than to rely on obedience and police-patrol his subordinates' work locations. He sets little store on his formal authority and power to penalize. He gets respect for skill in aiding people to participate in ways that permit them to see along with him the same moving-toward-completion scenario of what needs to be done.

• • •

In the Gateway Corporation, each regional manager and his assistant manager, together with headquarters staff, convene with that region's unit supervisors on an annual basis to develop objectives for the next year. There are eight main areas in which regional objectives are developed; unit performance, customer satisfaction, and so on.

At the annual meeting recently held the unit performance objective was discussed. From data on the past year's performances, it became evident there were a number of units identifiable as poor performers relative to the regional and national performance averages.

One of the supervisors, George Smallwood, noticed that in his own unit two of the data transmission facilities were below regional and national averages. In effect, they were making Deerton Region fall short of the overall objective to meet and, if possible, surpass national averages. It was agreed at the conclusion of the meeting that improvement efforts should be stepped up in the poorer performing sections. The supervisors would go back to their units and involve people in determining ways and means of improving the performances of these substandard facilities.

When George Smallwood arrived back at his unit, he got together with his group and reviewed with them the objectives that had been agreed upon in terms of accomplishments for the coming year. "The number one item, of course, is unit performance. In that connection, a problem we have is that two of our facilities are below regional and national averages. So to begin, let's discuss how their performance might be improved. Let's see how many ideas we can develop here as a first step toward getting this problem licked."

This kind of approach by George was not a sudden new departure for him. The technicians knew they could bring up ideas without risk of being rebuffed, put down, smoothed over, or ignored. Accordingly, as the members began thinking through the data transmission problem and possible solutions to it, an idea would be proposed and George would write it up. Frequently the growing list would spark off other team members' ideas. These included the proposal that George should discuss control line problems with the telephone company which provided the lines to these facilities. One of the technicians described how unreliable these lines were. In his judgment, "outages" were occurring because of vegetation getting into the lines and creating noise pulses which shut the facility down. Another member's suggestion was that through team effort, 100 percent of the routine maintenance should be accomplished on the two facilities. This had not been achieved during the past year. Someone else pointed out that commercial power to the data transmission installations had not been dependable. He suggested a visit with the power company to see if they could furnish more reliable power.

Through the combined team efforts, a number of additional improvements were identified. Individual and task-force assignments were agreed upon. By the end of the meeting, George and his team were clear about what they needed to do about improving facility performance. A detailed plan for doing so was now under development and would be checked out and finalized for implementation.

Before closing the meeting, George thanked his technicians for what they had contributed, remarking, "No single individual among us could have come up with such a comprehensive program for phasing out difficulties that have bugged us all this time. What we must have been doing before was firefighting on bits and pieces of the problem with data transmission. . . ."

"Now we've got it all together," someone commented enthusiastically.

• • •

This was a 9,9 team management approach in that the supervisor furnished his people with objectives that were important for the region to achieve. After outlining the big picture, he involved them by getting their ideas on how the two facilities' performance could be improved. Commitment on their part came about as they worked up the comprehensive solution through frank and creative discussion among all who, from up-front experience with data-transmission malfunctions, had ideas about how to get the big problem solved.

MANAGING MISTAKES AND ERRORS

Mistakes and errors are seen differently under a 9,9 approach than under other ways of supervision. Here's why.

A 9,9 supervisor realizes there are at least three general causes of mistakes and errors. The first is whenever subordinates don't have needed skills or background to carry out tasks. Mistakes can happen in any situation where people are eager to fulfill their objectives but at the same time don't know how. Often situations can be anticipated and prevented by specialized learning courses. When a mistake does happen, a 9,9 approach in the short term is on-the-job coaching in the "here and now." Beyond that, development requirements that are spotted are noted for the next round of setting objectives.

A more continuing answer to mistakes and errors relies on teamwork. Because 9,9-oriented team colleagues feel responsibility for one another, they can be expected to help anyone who is having difficulty by giving him the "how to do it" knowledge and skill on the spot.

A second cause of mistakes and errors arises from inadequate participation skills. Specifying and getting agreement on steps and procedures by which goals are to be accomplished takes a lot of thinking and analysis. The supervisor's desires can be 9,9, but to bring these values into daily work calls for good discussion skills. Less than clear understanding on the subordinate's part traces back to the boss. Possibly he was too hurried and was pushing the discussion along, glossing over points that subordinates thought they understood but didn't. Maybe at the time he failed to realize their need to probe more deeply into a problem. The correction here is for the boss to re-examine his leadership.

The 9,9 way of learning involves the use of _critique_: a process that involves comparing something with something else. Through such comparison, similarities and differences can be evaluated and judgments can be drawn—"This is better than that"—"This is good. That is bad"—"This is more efficient"— "Important—trivial." Once evaluative judgments have been drawn, one can ask, "So what?" or "What should we do about it?" At this point a range of alternatives are likely to spring to mind. On the other hand, this situation may be more complex and may require study to identify various possibilities of solution. Each alternative can be weighed and evaluated, pros and cons can be looked into, and one alternative compared with another until the best solution to solve this problem is reached and implemented. Inviting his subordinates to critique with him can help a supervisor see what is causing their difficulty. An essential pre-condition for effective critique discussions is that the authority of one person over others is not used to replace evidence and fact as the basis for insight. It means that open, candid comparisons, examination of differences and similarities, and resolution by mutual understanding are the conditions of learning. Given a 9,9-oriented boss who is working to create an open, free, and candid team situation, subordinates usually not only are very aware of where difficulties are located, but also are willing to speak up about them. They can tell him where blockages to their understanding came from and what he could do in the future to prevent such problems recurring.

Critique occurs in some after-the-fact situations and puts the spotlight on mistakes and errors. Many of these might have been anticipated before they occurred but weren't. Just as clearly, 9,9 is the only major style on the Grid that sees subordinate-to-supervisor critique as the right thing to do, in contrast with being taken as "rebellion" or just "blowing off steam" and so on. Genuine 9,9 self-development by the supervisor of himself as leader comes from the *learning* that results from a particular critique point. How is a supervisor to learn to do better if he doesn't know what needs improving? Once he knows, the mistake or error will not be made again.

If *you* are moving toward being a 9,9 supervisor and begin thinking of mistakes and errors in these terms, you might also notice that a third general source has been in operation. This is when you come to see that some errors, which are not traceable to insufficient knowledge and skill or to faulty understanding at the planning stage, may derive from boredom or worry. A point to check is whether a subordinate is being turned off by a job which poses much less challenge and success-through-accomplishment possibilities than he feels capable of responding to. Or it might be that his performance is being adversely affected by problems of which you are presently unaware.

• • •

Jim Stokes developed a habit of frequently using annual leave without pre-planning or scheduling. A typical instance would be when he called the supervisor during the first twenty minutes of the work day and gave some reason why he urgently needed to be on annual leave. In most cases this could have been avoided by advance planning on Jim's part.

The use of unscheduled leave by Jim was all too frequently placing a heavier work load on the other employees in his unit, and their hostility was beginning to show. The supervisor, Bob Bletchley, had brought up the unscheduled leave problem for discussion at team meetings. Here he had not judged it appropriate to name anyone, and neither had anyone else on Bob's team even though there had been some meaningful glares as others described examples of inconvenience. As Jim's request became more frequent, Bob had begun mentioning to Jim that he would appreciate more foresightedness and longer previous notice, but apparently Jim was not impressed.

Determined to crack the problem, Bob called Jim into his office. "Jim, let's discuss your use of unscheduled leave. First, here are the company's requirements." He pointed out that unscheduled leave is allowed when absolutely necessary but should not become routine. He explained that when frequent violation occurs, this makes it less possible for supervisors to pre-plan work schedules, productivity suffers, and the work load is increased for others. "In your particular case, Jim, it has come to the point where Jerry, Eloise and the others are having to work overtime which they don't want and are now beginning to resent very much, with focus on you."

"Whew!" Jim fidgeted. "I know they've turned hostile on me lately, but I hadn't figured just why. I used to enjoy working with these people, but the way they've been changing, what with all my other worries. . . ." He did a retake. "Look, Bob, I'll give it to you straight—I have a kind of disorganized family situation sometimes, which I won't go into detail about. Maybe if I make a real effort I can get it squared away. I'm going to try, and you can watch how the record shows from here on. But if, after a week, I get the sense of the family problem not clearing up, I'll let you know and then, well, maybe. . ."

"Go hit it for success first, Jim. Thank you for your commitment." Both stood up, they shook hands, and the interview ended.

• • •

This was a 9,9 approach by the supervisor because it began with Bob's first stating the problem from the organization's viewpoint and then relating this to the simultaneous *people* situation in which Jim's working colleagues were becoming more and more irked by the extra load his erratic absences imposed on them.

As the message registered with Jim, the effect on *him*—neither a premeditated nor an inevitable one, let it be noted—seems to have come first in the people area. It clarified what he had not previously grasped: *why* Jerry, Eloise and the others had been turning against him. Then came his mention of non-company connected worries. Bob did not probe into these. Instead, Jim took time to think, and then came up with a commitment offered to Bob that he would work hard on clearing up the family-related problems that had been a deepseated cause of his irregular use of annual leave.

To the degree boredom is a factor in causing mistakes and errors, perhaps your subordinate has not yet approached you directly about this. Or maybe he once did, either with you or some other boss, and got brushed off to his further frustration. Now his situation is well on the down side.

If facts are found to fit this kind of pattern, the 9,9 boss needs to get with the subordinate and work toward redesigning his job. In this way they can step up the challenge it could contain, and so put new interest into it. This is job enrichment. It's not a cosmetic facelift of an existing collection of ho-hum chores, but a personal development avenue for the individual who wants to "have at it" in testing his capabilities to contribute to organization purposes.

HANDLING COMPLAINTS

Complaints are significant to the 9,9 supervisor. Their expression is valued by him because they offer him the chance to deal with people "where they live." Frustrations, reservations, doubts, and disagreements about "what's going on that's less than okay" are evidence of problems that need to be dealt with so as to keep participation, involvement, and commitment high.

It was mentioned earlier that a 9,9 supervisor can learn from subordinates' critique how better to anticipate and so guide *himself* away from making the kinds of mistakes that reduce his effectiveness as a leader. What needs to be focused on now is the extent to which a complaint may or may not be critique.

It's largely a question of "What is the *real* problem?" To illustrate, you will recall that at a scheduled critique session, all team members are present. From the start, then, this makes for a different situation than the one where an individual member comes to the supervisor privately to voice a complaint. In the team situation a supervisor has more information sources to draw upon when an as yet unidentified "critique or complaints?" issue is raised. For example, Joe might launch into lengthy technical explanation to support his view that "The dam upstream is said to be about to burst, Harry; you're sleeping on the problem—we need action, but fast!" Harry, the supervisor, replies he hadn't known about the dam possibility. He asks if Joe has been upstream to check stresses and strains. Joe says no but adds he sure is worried. Harry then asks the others what they might know about Joe's concern. It could turn out that someone was up there the other day on an inspection visit looking for flaws but found none. That's not conclusive, of course. But it is evidence in the opposite direction from Joe's unsupported assertion. The evidence may be more vague and partly conflicting, as when some member says he flew over the dam recently and the lake was pretty full, but that's nothing unusual. Someone else says, "Look at the stream outside here—its level's way down—that could mean the spillway's gotten blocked and the dam's overloaded!" Harry and the others also see the implications, and a decision is soon taken to investigate at the scene. Joe's initial contribution wasn't much to go on. It sounded like one of those rumors that seem to have little relevance to the work situation and which people sometimes use as "handles" to express feelings rather than facts. Maybe it was, but the example also shows how other points of evidence can be researched out of the team members' knowledges so as to make at least a there-and-then determination of whether the complaint relates to a *real* problem. Where unidentified safety hazards are operating, this can make all the difference between prevention and post-mortem.

When a subordinate comes to the boss to voice a complaint, and only the two of them are present, there is seldom any immediate access to evidence "outside" the person himself. Granted that "confidentiality" can be overdone and abused under certain Grid styles, the 9,9 supervisor is careful to recognize when a complaint matter is private in the sense that it cannot be put into a team critique session's agenda. Given his high concerns *both* for production *and* people, however, the 9,9 supervisor will not accept without question as "private" a complaint that involves himself and/or other team members. He will say, "Look, let's neither of us be oversensitive personally about this issue, for there may be a problem here that is better to put on the table where everyone can take a look at it. Will you agree then, Joe, to bring this up at a critique meeting I'll convene as early as possible?"

This already is testing the *reality* of Joe's complaint which presently, as far as either he or his supervisor can tell, might be altogether different from the two "realisms" that Joe on the one hand is feeling from his insides and that on the other hand the supervisor is first observing from the outside.

It is possible for both persons to talk the problem through in the supervisor-subordinate interview. The option is for either to bring it up later in team critique session if he feels the problem would be better resolved there. In one-on-one discussions, what the 9,9 supervisor has to guard against is letting himself use his "position" to dictate or otherwise influence a reality that has not yet been examined. A 9,1 command decision such as "Quit complaining, Joe, and get back to work!" creates a new reality for this subordinate but has not dealt with "Joe coming to his supervisor with a complaint."

• • •

Gene Latta, a new first-line supervisor, had been promoted from the assembly-line work force at Alphabet Products. Like all promotions, his selection had drawn much comment and discussion among employees on the line. Gene had worked alongside nearly all of the people he was now supervising, knew them and their families by first names, and had fished, hunted, and camped with several of the guys.

One morning there was an incident with Bill Bruce. Gene had asked him to go to a different work station for 30 minutes in order to provide lunch relief. Bill did so, but later came back to Gene. He said, "You really think you're something—a new supervisor, pushing guys around. What makes you think you're a better man than me?"

Gene's 9,9 response to the situation was to take Bill aside in private and explain that his selection as the new supervisor was made by the management based on whatever grounds it had for finding him suitable to become a supervisor. Though it took two to make a relationship, Gene stressed, his own objective was to do the best job within his abilities, to treat all people fairly, and to get the job done.

Bill did a retake then and there. He looked at Gene and said, "Okay, I got the message. Frankly, I wanted to make line supervisor myself, and I still hope to do so. But between ourselves, Gene—and no apple-polishing intended—I did come unbuttoned in a way that was unfair to you, and I'm sorry."

"Re-button your lip, Bruce, or you'll have me crying," Gene quipped. Bill and he broke up laughing, and they went back to their jobs.

• • •

For a 9,9 supervisor, the *real* problem may or may not be what the subordinate is saying. But some part of it certainly has to do with his present feelings. The first step in identifying the problem is to help this person bring out his feelings. Those that are caused by deeper existing problems of communication can be remedied by providing needed information. Others can be helped by problem-solving sessions between you, the particular subordinate, and perhaps some other team member(s). Complaints that are more "objectively" realistic—that is, ones which clearly connect to malfunctions produced by technical and other procedures—can be resolved by the supervisor removing the causes responsible for them. Alternatively he can initiate corrective actions with his own boss for those changes needing higher approval before taking needed action.

So to sum up: a 9,9 supervisor doesn't treat a complaint as "just bellyaching," or as something to be soothed or ignored or cooled off. The complaint is a reality because it means that one or more subordinates are concerned about what's going on which is seen as wrong. The supervisor draws out the feelings first and then researches the factual aspects of the complaint. All the while he seeks to aid the subordinate to join in this process of examining what's being put on the table. This is how the entire problem can get cleared up so that it no longer stands in the way of committed effort.

REACTING TO HOSTILE FEELINGS

There are fewer occasions for a subordinate to feel hostile once the boss-subordinate relationship gets on a 9,9 footing. When a boss and subordinate are interacting on a mind-meeting basis, and continue to do so, then tensions that might expand into hostile feelings get resolved at each point along the way. They have little opportunity to build up.

But hostile feelings can still arise, particularly when the boss somehow gets seen, whether more or less accurately, as not entirely "being on the up-and-up" according to the unified 9,9 concerns. They must be dealt with. Bear in mind that subordinates will soon have some understanding of the Grid if not always of their own styles!

Here are the aspects of how a 9,9 boss reacts to hostile feelings. The concept is that hostile feelings, because they exist, are important. Because they are important, they need to be dealt with in a sound manner, and if the boss is ready to change those aspects of his behavior that may be unaligned with 9,9 as well as having been the cause of hostile feelings, boss-subordinate relationships can be strengthened and two main benefits result. One is better productivity. The other is a subordinate who is

ready to participate more strongly and to give his involvement
and commitment.

• • •

Ron Snell, a factory foreman, rushed into his boss' office and
yelled, "What's gotten into you, Harry? You've made a fool of
me in front of all my people and that shop steward"

"Tell me what I did, Ron, and we'll look into it." Harry was
surprised by the sudden outburst—he had never seen Ron in
this state before—but did not feel indignant about it or anxious.
He indicated the chair by his desk, and the supervisor sat down,
still fuming.

"You've taken his side and reversed me on that Clampett
affair—why?"

"I've got the papers right here and a meeting scheduled with
the head steward at eleven to go over the case. As yet, I've
made no decision one way or the other, far less announced
anything without subbing you in before it reached Mrs. Clampett."

"Riley's bragging that he's won!"

"Then he's out of line—that grievance is still on the table between Hughes and me, and we'll start discussing it in a couple
of hours' time."

"You've let him go over my head, anyway."

"No, Ron; as shop steward he's exercised one of his options
and independently passed it up for Hughes to handle with me.
I was going to touch base with you before the meeting, so now
you're here, let's take a look at her grievance."

"As I told her and Riley, it's ridiculous!"

"That's one way of responding to a grievance—do you think
it's the best?"

"Knock it off, Harry, you know the election's next month and
Riley's trouble-making to build his image. Hughes too, I think."

"Ron, what I *do* know is that under our agreed procedure a
department's supervisor and the shop steward are first required
to carry out a joint investigation of the facts and try to agree on
a solution. If they can't reach a joint decision, they can at least

agree to disagree, put their facts and points of disagreement down on paper, and refer it up as a *joint submission* to Hughes and me."

Harry paused, then added, "Now, that hasn't happened in the Clampett case; and from the tone of your 'it's ridiculous' remark it's not surprising that Riley seems to have concluded that no joint investigation was feasible. Anyway, there's been a solo referral by Riley, and as usual, Hughes is likely to come to this 11:00 a.m. meeting very well briefed to argue Mrs. Clampett's case. So far, all *I've* got is your one-liner on the supervisor's statement: 'Mrs. Clampett's performance does not warrant upgrading her hourly rate!' "

Ron fidgeted. "Alright, sorry, I'm no good at writing things out, but I'll tell you all you'll need as proof to send Hughes packing."

"I'd feel better prepared if I could see her grievance from more than one side—you know, Ron, the kind of pros and cons that get set out in a joint supervisor-steward submission. So why don't we do something to make up for that missing joint investigation?" Harry buzzed his secretary for Mrs. Clampett's personnel file and output records, and announced, "I'm going to be devil's advocate for a little while as we look into this grievance and explore for a best solution. Let's go, Ron, what are the facts?—show me!"

• • •

It was hard sledding to begin with, but Harry persevered with the roleplay and not only drew out the briefing information he required but at the same time provided Ron with a training experiment in investigating the facts of a specific grievance jointly with a shop steward and attempting to resolve differences, rather than either or both persons seizing and defending partisan positions in a spreading dispute.

This handling of Ron's reaction was 9,9 in that Harry found out what the problem and its causes were, made Ron aware of how he'd aborted department-level grievance handling, and in a timely fashion innovated a training experience for the prejudiced supervisor as well as securing information that he, Harry, would need for the upcoming grievance session with Mrs. Clampett and the head steward. Homer was made aware, too, that better grievance investigation and settlement on his part at the department level would help prevent unnecessary "summit conferences" such as this one.

A 9,9 boss like Harry recognizes that hostile feelings are a symptom something is not okay. This means that the boss doesn't see the subordinate as "bad" or "no good" because he has hostile feelings. His first desire is to know what it is that is not okay. One approach for finding out is to be open with his subordinate. To be open means to communicate to the subordinate that he really wants to understand what is causing the friction. It means that the subordinate can talk freely because the boss is not going to tag him out for the first negative thing he says. The boss' goal is to avoid being judgmental. He's not neutral in the 1,1 way but is trying to stay as objective as he can within what can be a highly provoking emotional atmosphere as his subordinate sounds off in hostile fashion.

His staying open and nonjudgmental aids the subordinate to want to talk about the tensions he feels. When the boss can keep himself from feeling threatened by hostile feelings, he can listen to what is being said. The boss doesn't have his earplugs in. Neither does he adopt the attitude of, "As soon as he's had his say, I'll tell him where he's wrong."

Being open invites openness. Reacting without defensiveness invites nondefensive talking. Listening to what the subordinate says invites this subordinate to listen to what the boss will later say.

PERFORMANCE EVALUATION

If hostile feelings, as discussed above, have been worked through so that the boss-subordinate relationship is a good one, it is then possible for them to tackle a performance review or evaluation discussion without all of the roadblocks and barriers that otherwise might exist in the situation and be maneuvered around.

102

When supervision is through goals and objectives that are being achieved by individuals within 9,9 overall team action, it becomes possible to deal with performance evaluation by boss and subordinate studying together strengths and weaknesses that enabled goals and objectives to be reached or succeeded, or that prevented them from being met. In the latter case they can take steps to avoid them.

• • •

Sam Baker, head of Payroll Section, sat in his office reviewing his thoughts about the scheduled annual review of perform-ance with his secretary, Mary Smith, that was to take place today. He had informed Mary two weeks ago that he had marked this specific time on his calendar to discuss her per-formance-evaluation report for the past year.

Sam felt well prepared for the impending interview. He was confident not only about the accuracy of his ratings but also of his and Mary's well established and mostly common knowledges of the grounds on which these ratings had been made. During the past year they had talked five or six times about her per-formance. At one point he had told her, citing the evidence, that she was spending too much time in private conversation on the telephone, not only blocking the availability of that tele-phone for business use, but losing time that should be devoted to her work assignments. Sometime back, also, Sam had been dissatisfied with her spelling. Having discussed both these im-provement areas with Mary, they had agreed upon a set of standards that both felt were attainable by her. Since then sub-stantial progress had been made, particularly on the telephone problem. Additional work was required in the spelling area and Sam had made some comments on Mary's review form regard-ing this.

At precisely three o'clock, Mary looked in to inquire, "Ready to interview, boss?" Sam invited her in and asked the other secretary to hold his calls until he and Mary had completed their conference. They then sat down at the table, away from his desk, to discuss the rating form. Neither felt at all tense about the project before them.

Mary pulled out a list. "I've brought along suggestions I'd like to talk about, not only to improve my efficiency, but the efficiency of the office."

"Well, thanks, Mary. Do you think we ought to start with this?"

"Oh, no; later would be better, after we've been through the review itself."

"Okay, so here it is for you to look through and we can discuss any points you'd like to make. Generally, I'm very happy with your work. I feel you've made considerable progress in the areas we discussed previously. In 'Writing Skill' here, I think you still need to improve your letter composition and spelling. Over here, under 'Development,' I've recommended that you take a refresher course in this area, maybe at night school, or through a home study course if one's available."

Mary studied Sam's ratings and written comments for some minutes and then signed her section of the form and said, "Mr. Baker, I'm satisfied with the report. In a few areas I'm not satisfied with myself, and I'm going to try to improve in each of them. Now, here are these other improvements I think can be made with your help."

They then looked at the list Mary had pulled out earlier. Sam was impressed with her suggestions for improved filing techniques, and how Sam's own method of dictation could be improved. These were discussed and agreed upon.

• • •

This is a 9,9 approach to performance evaluation because Sam had taken the responsibility of an ongoing performance review program seriously and had discussed Mary's performance with her several times prior to making his annual evaluation. In doing so, Mary and Sam have established a good rapport. They understand what the standards are and they have a set of objectives for improving her performance.

Additionally, informing Mary of the impending review two

weeks in advance gave proper weight and consideration to the process and provided time for both Sam and Mary to prepare themselves for the interview.

This kind of solid footing has several advantages. One is that boss and subordinate may conclude that the goals and objectives that were set were unrealistically high. Forward planning, however detailed, has its limits in the inevitable "view" from the here-and-now. Even the best forecast can indicate "a light at the end of the tunnel" which turns out, as one gets nearer, to be a will-o'-the-wisp. 9,9 performance review will check the pros and cons of this. The accomplishment actually turned in may be judged as excellent, even though it failed to meet the objectives themselves. On the other hand, it may turn out that the goals and objectives set were so low that the subordinate was not challenged to "reach." This says that the subordinate's performance was judged to be of high quality, but that in the future his goals should aim at higher accomplishments. Sometimes goals and objectives are realistically high and a number of reasons are responsible for their not being reached. Again, the reason for this can be from many sources. Whatever the cause, however, it is important that it be identified so that corrective action can be taken in the period ahead.

There are other possibilities, of course.

A few examples can indicate the direction of thinking. One is the subordinate has slumped into a 1,1 attitude. Under these conditions his private strategy is to do the minimum necessary to get by. He avoids giving his involvement and commitment because he just doesn't want to be bothered. Or, it may be that the subordinate's Grid style is 5,5. Rather than being prepared to set high goals of excellence, he gives them no more than lip service. He takes the tempo from those he works around or from others outside his unit. Then what he does is about like what is being called for by others. Such a standard in many organizations is nothing less than mediocre. Alternatively, the subordinate's attitude might be 9,1 or 1,9.

What a boss does in performance appraisal depends on the

Grid style with which the subordinate approaches the situation. The boss' task is to talk with the subordinate in Grid terms, giving him feedback to enable him to see himself in the framework of the Grid. Then the subordinate can see his behavior in terms that he previously had not paid attention to. Then if the boss has supervisory skills, he can do much to aid a subordinate to shift his Grid style, not only by pointing out what the problem is, but by working with him on a daily basis and assisting him to shift from his "natural" style of approach to standards of excellence. The problem may be a matter of knowledge or skill. That means the subordinate is being called upon to do things he is not prepared to do. Then the boss' task is to help design a personal study project, to give him further on-the-job coaching, or to enroll him in special training courses that will permit him to overcome deficiencies.

Clarity in all these and much else is helped or hindered to the extent that the boss himself is operating according to 9,9. Who needs a 5,5 boss, who has self-deceived himself that he's 9,9, advising one on how to perform better? Not only is the advice miscalibrated, the supervisor himself is a source of bad vibrations that put your teeth and others' nerves on edge.

Still another possibility is that the subordinate is in over his head. He is attempting to do a job for which he does not have the capability or skill, and where knowledge enrichment would not help either. Then the boss talks with the subordinate in terms of reassignment to an activity which will create less pressure on him and permit him to do a better job. There are other possibilities, but the above gives the trend of thinking. To sum up, performance evaluation serves the purpose of aiding boss and subordinate to set challenging goals and objectives. Its other purpose is to identify causes of poor performance that have blocked objectives from being reached, and to set in motion various courses of action that can help those deficiencies to be eliminated.

SUMMARY

The 9,9 approach is based on involvement, participation, and commitment. It calls for a different kind of boss-subordinate interaction than is found in other Grid locations.

1. Communication is an open, candid, free exchange between boss and subordinate. Neither needs to be on his guard in order to avoid risking misunderstanding by the other.

2. Directions are not "given" on a task-by-task basis except under unique emergency or last-resort circumstances. Directions arise from work goals and objectives on which boss and subordinate already have agreed. The subordinate can operate on a more or less self-regulated basis.

3. Mistakes and errors are viewed from the standpoint of background causes responsible for them. The view toward taking corrective actions is to eliminate the causes.

4. Complaints may arise from any number of sources, but the important point in 9,9 supervision is that the complaint be understood and dealt with. This can be done either by eliminating whatever has caused the complaint or expanding the information of the person complaining. Where he was misinformed, he is now better informed, and the problem fades from his mind permanently rather than being temporarily put at rest by a soothing statement.

5. Reacting to hostile feelings takes as its basis the view that hostile feelings indicate problems in the work situation. Hostile feelings are a danger signal. A 9,9 boss reacts to them in a very serious-minded way. He works to understand them through open, candid, authentic interaction with the subordinate under nonjudgmental, nondefensive conditions so that genuineness of communication can occur. Then corrective actions can be taken to eliminate causes responsible for hostile feelings.

6. 9,9 performance evaluation relates performance to previously-set goals and objectives. In this way, performance evalua-

tion takes place on an objective level. It becomes possible for the boss to help the subordinate see what has caused him to excel in objectives as set, or to miss them by whatever margin. If the objectives set are realistically high and they have been missed, then counseling is undertaken to stimulate better performance in the future. If the person's competence is inadequate to the goals, then the problem is one of reassignment.

CHAPTER 7

Implications

As stated before, authority-obedience is on the way out. Accepted almost without question for many centuries, it seems to have passed some point of no return in the late 1960s.

Authority-obedience supervision is 9,1 supervision. As bosses backed off from 9,1 because it no longer worked well for them, many shifted to a 5,5 compromise, accommodation, adjustment, "half-loaf" approach. As a result, and not surprisingly, we see everywhere a deterioration in the work ethic. Product and service quality isn't what it used to be. Absenteeism, tardiness, sick leave, and a host of other ways of escaping work, including long coffee breaks, unnecessary conferences, and so on, all point to the same conclusion. Such attitudes toward work are neither productive in terms of organization results nor gratifying in terms of personal satisfaction.

But not all supervisors opted for the 5,5 approach. Other supervisors looking for alternatives to 9,1 shifted over to a sweetness and light 1,9 way or a see no evil, speak no evil 1,1 approach. A few tried hop-scotching around the Grid, doing whatever they thought subordinates expected or would accept —being nice with a 1,9 subordinate, ignoring a 1,1, playing the organization-man game with 5,5ers, and being tough with 9,1 subordinates. Before the Grid was introduced as a way of strengthening supervision, there were a few bosses who were able to unify high production and people concerns and achieved

9,9 relationships, getting shared understanding and agreement on solution-seeking ways of problem solving through involvement, participation, and commitment from those they supervised.

THE CONSEQUENCES OF FOUR DIFFERENT WAYS OF SUPERVISING

Different supervisory styles have different implications, according to the outcomes they produce. 9,1's unrelenting emphasis on results at all costs causes a supervisor to ramrod his people to get their jobs done. He is quick to place blame but slow to praise, always ready to issue orders to people but seldom disposed to sit down with a person who is having difficulty and coach him toward proficiency. Day after day, as he radiates disapproval of their actions and skepticism about their brainpower and their intentions, his subordinates become more convinced that it's an undesirable place to work. It is a hard, weary, and resentment-loaded struggle to maintain one's personal stability and dedication under this kind of supervision, for the perpetual message is, "You're always wrong, you're too dumb to make it, all you do is waste time and make mistakes."

1,9 has its consequences also, but in a strikingly different way. The 1,9 supervisor is very conscious of his subordinates' feelings; always making sure they are content. He wants to be accepted and liked and therefore ensures his subordinates are accommodated. The effects of this approach combine and accumulate. Some subordinates become irritated by its shallowness and the lack of attention to solving profit-reducing problems. Others respond to this affectionate warmth. In effect, the supervisor is providing a flight from maturity and other demands of the real world. Seeing that, other subordinates become even more frustrated. Can teamwork develop here? More important, the "weak" stay because it's secure; the "strong" leave because it's stifling.

1,1 is supervision in name only. Subordinates may think the boss is an easy person to work for because he "lets us think

for ourselves." But after they have found themselves in difficult situations produced by the boss' negligence, impressions
change. Subordinates begin to wonder, "What's that character
doing in charge of us? Who needs *him*?" Morale suffers. The
next higher boss is likely to find himself taking charge of problems on a "bypass" basis.

5,5 supervision carries its own unique implications which
emerge as time passes. Most come as side effects of the "balancing act" and the "half a loaf is better than none" aspects of
the approach. An uneasy though apparently "controlled" level
of discontent persists because subordinates can see *some* but
less than gratifying progress being made in results and people
areas. Some who work under 5,5 supervision come to doubt
that a bureaucratic or "organization man" mentality can solve
the fundamental problems that must be grappled with. Other
subordinates take their theme from the supervisor and assume
that things are going as well as can be expected under the circumstances. Basically it depends on how content a person can
be with mediocrity. Unchallenged by work, subordinates' interests turn to company politics; or, avocational interests come
to have an exaggerated pull on thoughts and feelings.

As a sound approach to supervision, 9,9 is most in accord
with developmental insights from behavioral science theory. It
is an "open" approach that promotes teamwork toward better
results. There are several keys to it. It means setting high standards for excellence in performance and helping subordinates
get there. It means using critique to check out past efforts to
see how to deal with new problems in a better way. An overriding clue is dignity and respect for your subordinate. What
this means is that you *listen*. If you agree, you acknowledge his
contribution. If you disagree and he's right, you acknowledge
your error. If you disagree and deadlock, you look for the real
cause of the misunderstanding. As indicated throughout the
book, it means a lot more, but these are basic.

Though supervising in a 9,9 way may mean more production
for the organization and more rapid advancement for yourself,

the real motivation for striving in a 9,9 direction is that it is a sound, human way to move into the future.

CAN A SUPERVISOR CHANGE?

Yes, a supervisor can change. The real question is, "How can such change be brought about?"

There are at least four conditions that are desirable for bringing about real change toward 9,9.

The first is that supervisors know theories of sound and unsound behavior. When you have a clear understanding of Grid theory, you have the possibility of seeing new options, alternatives, and possibilities that otherwise would be outside your field of vision. Theory points out how 9,1 works, what 1,9 is, how 1,1 goes, and the techniques of getting along in a 5,5 way. It also provides clear indications for what a 9,9 basis of teamwork leadership requires of the supervisor and this is not easy. Then you can understand what you need to do to change.

The second condition is that you are clear in seeing yourself. This means you strip away self-deception and are able to look at your own behavior, calling a spade a spade. That is, you do not kid yourself, saying that your approach is 9,9 when really it is 9,1; you do not confuse 5,5 organization-man attitudes with 9,9 team achievement. You don't rationalize to yourself that 1,9 sweetness and light is really the way of getting people involved in work. You don't delude yourself into believing that 1,1 is an okay way to settle for an easy time when you look at all the blockages that you have to contend with.

The third condition for a person changing is that he sees a gap between where he is and what he would like to become as a supervisor. It means that a person who's a 9,1 not only can see that but also can see 9,9 as a practical ideal. It means that a person who is in a 1,9 attitude can see that he will not lose the sought-after warmth and affection of people if he challenges his subordinates to meaningful and significant accomplishments. It means that a 1,1-oriented supervisor recognizes that a loser's career won't be much to look back on, and that he has a job to do. It means that a 5,5-oriented person comes to see that "splitting the difference" compromise is a weak instrument of mediocrity. In other words, a person needs to see the gap between what he sees as his own way of supervising and what he recognizes to be a better way to supervise.

The fourth condition of change is that people around you in the environment of work give you their support and help you change. This means that the bosses know and value efforts toward becoming 9,9. It means that colleagues do the same and that subordinates who are *getting* support respond to it and contribute to the teamwork. People around you give necessary encouragement when things get tough. They give you clues when you are in a blind alley. They give you recognition when you're accomplishing what everyone has come to recognize as really top-notch.

IS 9,9 A PRACTICAL IDEAL?

Some would argue that 9,9 is too idealistic; that as an everyday practical reality it can't be achieved by people who work together. Too often before, when you've been at your wit's end, your boss pressuring for results, there seemed no option other than cracking down for a result or opting out of supervision altogether. A way of testing this is to answer the question, "How would it have been possible for the supervisors depicted in this book to have solved the problems in a 9,9 way?" Every example presented could have been handled in a 9,9 way. The challenge of excellence in supervision is to recognize and act on the 9,9 possibility rather than settling for something less.